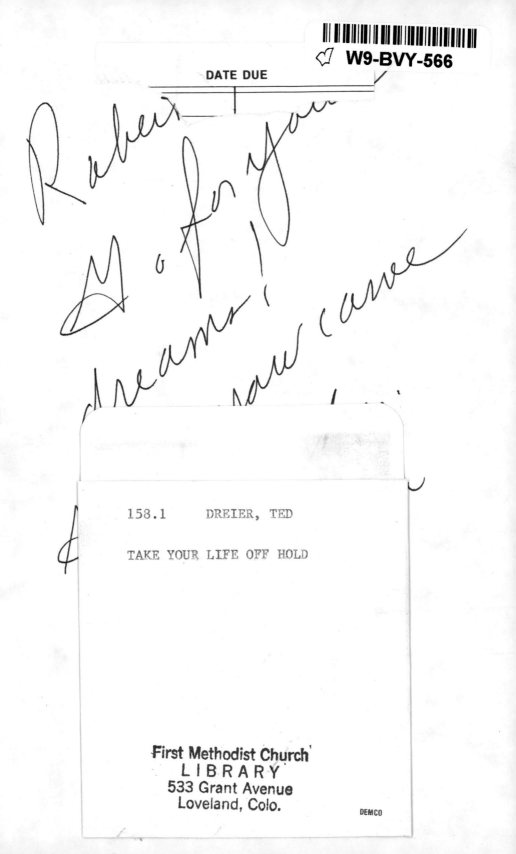

375

Take Your LIFE OFF HOLD

Ted Dreier

Fulcrum, Inc.
Golden, Colorado

Book and Jacket Design by Linda Seals

Library of Congress Cataloging-in-Publication Data

Dreier, Ted
Take Your Life Off Hold

Bibliography: p.
1. Conduct of life. I. Title
BJ1581.2.D74   1987   158'.1   87-12065
ISBN 1-55591-020-3

2 3 4 5 6 7 8 9 0

Printed in the United States of America

For . . .

. . . my parents, Kenneth and Velma Dreier,
   who allowed me to explore life as a child.

. . . my wife Karen,
   who has been very supportive in our lifestyle change.

. . . our two sons, Kent and Kyle,
   who encouraged their parents to "go for it."

. . . and Bernice Anderson
   who, at the age of 92, continues to inspire me
   about what it means to lead a full life.

ACKNOWLEDGMENTS

A special thanks to the 89 people who gave up time from their businesses and family lives for me to interview them. I appreciate their openness in expressing feelings and answering delicate questions that they hadn't been asked before. We all gain from their sharing of life experiences.

Thanks to friends for their interest and questions that gave me fresh stimulation while writing this book.

Thanks to 92-year-old Bernice Anderson who read through the material and shared insights from her experience as a writer–and continually reminded me that I should use *who* when referring to people and *that* when referring to things.

Thanks to Sean Schneider, a local bookstore manager, for his encouragement and assistance in reading over the manuscript.

Thanks to businessman David Olmstead for his interest in the topic and his role as devil's advocate, which helped me become more aware of how readers might misinterpret my thoughts.

Thanks to Darby Junkin for her editorial comments— pointing out those pages where the writing felt mechanical or lacked feeling and energy.

Thanks to my wife, Karen, for her assistance in helping transcribe the taped interviews, for her responses when I yelled over my shoulder, "How do you spell . . . ?" for her reading the original printouts and telling me when she felt I needed to start over again, for her understanding as she saw me glued to the word processor day after day or leaving for another interview.

Thanks to you readers who are interested in what I have to say in this book.

CONTENTS

INTRODUCTION

WHY?

If you feel stuck, frustrated, burned out, or confused about what to do next, then you have come to the right book.

Are you anticipating tomorrow while putting what you really want to do with your life on hold today? All these tomorrows strung together become your life.

Many people painfully reflect on their lives thinking, "I wish I had done this; I wish I had done that." They realize their lives are on hold; they lack direction and motivation to achieve the happiness they want right now.

Then there are others like Lyle and Bernice Anderson who, in their late 60s, left the comfort of their Kansas farm home and went to Malawi, Central Africa to head the Cooperative Development Program which assisted village people in agricultural methods. Or, John Feight, who left his position with a major advertising firm to pursue his interest in art—and established the Foundation for Hospital Art. These people represent the increasing number of Americans who are focusing on quality of life, not just quantity.

In a front-page article, January 9, 1987, the *Wall Street Journal* referred to the number of people who are not waiting until 65 to quit their jobs. "According to the General Accounting Office, an agency of Congress, 17% of men and 7% of women between the ages of 55 and 61—some 1.9 million people in all—received pension benefits in 1983, the latest year for which government data are available. The count doubled over ten years." Cited in the article was Roger Birk, past

1

chairman and chief executive of Merrill Lynch & Co., who ended 30 years with the brokerage house in July 1985 at the age of 55. "I don't think we're put on this earth to make all the money we can," Birk said. "There are other ways you can live happily."

"What am I going to do with the rest of my life?" is a common question, according to Phillip Moffitt, president and editor-in-chief of *Esquire* magazine. In the December 1986 issue he responded, "A new generation of people are now in their forties and they can see ahead to what they are likely to obtain in income and achievement levels. What is happening with the individuals, like my friends, is that they are realizing it is in their interest to sacrifice some economic payoff for more general satisfaction with their lives. It may appear to be naive or somehow overly idealistic, but it is really a 'bottom line' type of computation, which measures net happiness rather than net dollars."

As I have discovered from my interviews, this revelation is not limited to those in their 40s. The need for fulfillment crosses all ages.

The inspiration for this book came from a major lifestyle change made by my wife, Karen, and me. Our change was not an easy decision. It was made with much thought. We felt strong tugs to stay put and other tugs to change.

Karen and I had lived in Irving, Texas, a Dallas suburb, for 17 years. Irving had played an important part in our lives. We had reared two boys there, made some very special friends and were very active in our local church. While we had enjoyed a full life there, both of our boys, Kent, 24, and Kyle, 20, were in college and we were beginning to feel stuck in a lifestyle that was missing something. The process of change began with my selling the business I had started 15 years earlier. This was followed by selling our four-bedroom house with pool, our furniture and most of the things we had collected during 25 years of marriage. Then we shipped only 22 medium-sized cardboard boxes of personal items to our condominium in Breckenridge, Colorado.

This lifestyle change made me curious about why others had made changes and how they felt about them. Did they get the same surprised and questioning looks from their friends? Did they experience the same fears we did? What advice would they have for others thinking about making lifestyle changes? Were they glad they had done it?

To answer these and other questions, I conducted in-depth interviews with 89 people from such places as Wichita, New York, Los Angeles, Houston, Dallas, Phoenix, Tampa, Minneapolis, Boston, Chicago, and Cleveland. There were people also from less-well-known places, all with a common goal of living a life with greater fulfillment. The focus of this book is not where people came from or where they moved to, but rather, the emotions, struggles and excitement they experienced as they made lifestyle changes.

Of the 89 people interviewed, 66 had actually made lifestyle changes while the other 23 were interviewed for their feelings about reactions to change. Of the 23, 11 had made major occupational changes at one time in their lives and six were professional counselors who had worked with people going through change. Of the 66 people who made lifestyle changes, 41 were married, 14 were single women and 11 were single men. Ages ranged from 24 to 72. I hope that from this broad spectrum of people with a variety of backgrounds and emotions, there will be many with whom you can identify in your search for taking your life off hold.

While most people I interviewed said they were happy to have their names used, others, for various reasons, preferred to be kept anonymous. I have honored their requests by using fictitious first names and not giving any last names. People introduced with first and last names are using their real names. In all cases, the settings and circumstances are as they were reported.

When people discovered I was writing a book, they had all kinds of questions and thoughts on the subject. People we meet in everyday settings become our teachers. Sometimes it's one sentence that grabs our attention; other times it's a lengthy sharing of experiences. As my mother used to tell me, "When the student is ready, the teacher appears"—and we are all students of life.

Most of those interviewed were making lifestyle changes that helped them slow down and smell the roses. Although most of them also made geographic moves, this is not necessary to make a lifestyle change. Rather, you may be dealing with the quality of your life—feeling that you are stuck and not doing what you would like to be doing. In fact, the change that you are searching for might include a more intense lifestyle, longer working hours, greater challenges. Regardless of the nature of your change, I hope you will find the tools and thoughts of those interviewed to be enlightening and helpful in taking your own life off hold.

There is a freshness to the life experiences of those who have risked change. They have gained personal confidence, an openness to new opportunities, an awareness of being present in the present.

In discussing lifestyle changes with other people, some said, "I would like to change, but don't know where to start." To meet that need, I have included specific questions, activities and exercises related to change; they have helped others— as well as me.

A number of lifestyle changes in my own life helped me to better understand the people I interviewed for this book. My first big change came as a teenager when my parents decided to sell our dairy farm. All of a sudden my career plans changed from farming to going to college to become a teacher. The second change came when Karen and I went to teach in Malawi, Central Africa, for three years—1962 to 1965. The third change occurred when I went into business for myself in 1971; the most recent change occurred in 1986. Each of these changes expanded my view of the endless opportunities available to all of us.

Making a lifestyle change is more than an event. It is an attitude that allows you to feel comfortable about changing your way of living as your values and priorities change. The alternative? Allowing yourself to stay stuck even after your priorities change.

If I were to write each of you a personal note it would say:

Dear Reader,

Congratulations on taking time to invest in your life. Your reading of this book tells me you are interested in the quality of life, not just the quantity. You realize your uniqueness and potential for living a fuller life.

As you read, breathe in the fears, excitement and insights of the experiences shared with you. Allow each person's experiences to give you courage to take your own life off hold.

You have only one life to live. It's up to you. I hope this book will help you laugh more, love more and be inspired to grab life with both hands.

Thanks,

Ted Dreier
Breckenridge, Colorado
September, 1987

IN SEARCH OF FULFILLMENT

Do you feel that there's got to be more to life? Do you feel stuck? If you only had six months to live, would you like to be doing what you are doing now? Are you earning more and more and it's still not enough? Do you feel like you are on an endless treadmill, running faster and faster, only to end each day feeling that something is missing?

So did Mitch and Ellen Pretner.

The painful realization of being caught in an endless rat race caused Ellen, 30, a successful paralegal, and Mitch, 29, a stockbroker, to make a lifestyle change. While they enjoyed their luxurious standard of living in Houston, and while Mitch was known as the best-dressed broker in the firm, they weren't fulfilled. "We knew there had to be more to life," was Mitch's feeling, "so we started exploring other opportunities and ended up buying a pizza restaurant in a beautiful little mountain town."

Mitch and Ellen are now experiencing life with a fresh perspective. Having made this lifestyle change, they can more clearly see the rut they were caught in. Like Mitch and Ellen, a growing number of Americans are evaluating their current lifestyles and exploring other options for greater fulfillment.

Teresa Bressert, 44, and her husband, Walter, found that their multi-million-dollar business was no longer fun. They were putting in 18-hour days, but their efforts were feeling less and less fruitful. "We saw our quality of life slipping away," said Teresa. "We were living under pretense—pretending that things were okay. When we took a serious look at our quality of life, we decided to make a change. We had to tell ourselves the truth."

Are you living a life clouded by pretense? If so, has this put your life on hold? Do you feel that something is missing from your life but you are not sure what?

David Winner, 33, a hairdresser from Boston, was making good money, yet something was missing. "I was making four times more than my father had ever made, but I still didn't feel successful." So David moved from Boston to a small town of 1,000. "Now I feel more of a blending of both sides of my life— a blending of nature and work." While David is working harder to make ends meet today, his change has given him more time to enjoy the beauty and serenity of nature.

Family concerns motivated Paul and Julie Mattos, both in their late 20s, to leave their good jobs in Silicon Valley and move to a setting where they could spend more time with their daughter. "What was important to us was we wanted to be closer to our three-year-old daughter, Shannon," Julie said. "Since we were both employed, it was a 90-mile trip each day to take Shannon to a babysitter I could trust. Now we both have more time to be with her."

The 66 people interviewed for this book who made life-style changes gave a variety of reasons for making the change— job-related frustrations, health problems, family considerations. Others reached a point of such frustration that they decided to make a change before they got any older. Regardless of the reasons for change, everyone's ultimate goal was the same: they wanted lives with greater fulfillment. What would motivate you to take *your* life off hold?

Karen and I made our lifestyle change because we wanted to invest more time in developing our interests —Karen with her art, music and handicrafts, and I with writing. While living in the Dallas Metroplex, we had gotten to the point that although we felt as if we were peddling as fast as we could, something was missing from our lives.

During the interviews, I found others had struggled with some of the same feelings. As they reminisced, I could relate to what they were saying because I had experienced similar feelings of uncertainty, fear, excitement. People spoke of skepticism from surprised friends. They also told how the change gave them a new lease on life, more energy, more excitement about the future, more personal confidence. Some admitted having wanted to make a change earlier, yet had kept pushing it back in their minds until one day something snapped and got them off dead center.

Each interview brought another thread of understanding to the complex fabric of change. By comparing individual differences and similarities, the main issues of change began to surface—issues such as the relationship between success and fulfillment.

STANDARDIZED SUCCESS DOESN'T BRING INDIVIDUALIZED FULFILLMENT

Success, in its many varied forms, becomes a god that captures our devotion. Some people sacrifice their lives for it. While being successful takes on the appearance of happiness and fulfillment, it can also be just the opposite. How? By trying to dance to someone else's tune instead of your own. You are a unique individual; your expectation of success is also unique. To assume that success is the same for everyone leads to major personal confusion and frustration.

Have you ever been waiting to see a certain movie and along comes a friend who advises you to see another movie that he/she describes as the best movie ever? You give up your movie, and the other movie turns out to be terrible—in your opinion. Remember how you wanted to kick yourself for not following through on your original plans?

The same thing can happen if you allow someone else to decide what is right for your life. You give up your uniqueness to mass thinking. Your journey is filled with the frustration of things just not seeming to fit into place. You are attempting to live by standardized success, which may not meet your unique needs. In deciding what you really want, focus on what is important to you—not on what someone else thinks. Live your own life.

Recognize that your desires change. What was important to you at one time may no longer be important. I used to think

I wanted a red Corvette. Now the thought of stuffing my 6'3"
body into such a small space sounds like work. Do you remember what was important to you 10 years ago? How has that
changed?

Eighteen years ago, I was struggling between getting a
master's degree in high school guidance counselling or one in
business administration. I was 30 years old with a wife and two
kids. I had decided that if I was going to get another degree, now
was the time. Having been an admissions counselor at Bethel
College in Kansas for three years, I had worked with a number
of high school counselors—and their work looked interesting.
On the other hand, I had been in the field of education since
college and was looking for a different environment. Another
consideration was that the money was better in business. Lots
and lots of lists were made in trying to decide what to do.
Business won.

After getting my master's in business from Wichita State,
I was ready to move from rural Kansas to a big city. Back then,
success for me was to get into a big company, make lots of
money and live in a big city with exciting things going on.
Moving to Dallas was exciting with its night life, major golf
tournaments and lots of dynamic people weaving their way up
the corporate hierarchy. I didn't like golf, but I loved the
excitement of being there.

Today, that conception of success and happiness has been
replaced by what some would call a simpler, more laid-back,
more quality-focused lifestyle. Yet there are millions of people
across the United States, including our 20- and 24-year-old
sons, who are striving to be upwardly mobile. To them, that is
quality living and success.

Success took on a new meaning for Dean and Jean Gray
after Dean's heart attack. The Grays, in their mid-50s, left
Elgin, Illinois, and made a major lifestyle change. Prior to the
heart attack, success to Dean meant getting all the overtime he
could. "During the recuperation from my heart attack, Jean and
I took long walks and did a lot of talking. What had been so
important to us at one time was no longer significant. We
discovered the intensity of our past lifestyle was keeping us
from enjoying the moment. It was during that time that I left

the company after 31 years and we moved to a resort town where we manage a condominium."

Jean added, "We discovered that success was not the accumulation of more but, rather, enjoying each day to the fullest. We used to look forward to the weekends, but now the whole week is like a weekend. To us this is success—to enjoy each moment to its fullest."

For some, success is power. It is getting an important title, having a big office with views on two sides, having a private secretary and a key to the executive washroom. To others, it is rearing a family that is respected by the community, a family where all the kids have gone on to college and then found good jobs. Others describe success as having a job that gives four weeks vacation every year. What would you add to the list?

At one time, success for Jeff Terrill, 45, meant having his boss's job. That changed. Jeff had been going up the corporate ladder at Western Airlines where he was vice president of route planning. He remembers sitting in his office, facing the pages of work and crises inherent in his job. When he thought of his boss's job, he realized, "There was nothing about it that I wanted—even though it would mean more pay. I knew what it was like to get promotions and more money. I love nice things, but I knew there had to be more."

In 1981, Jeff and his wife, Bunny, who was an assistant to a vice president, left their combined income of $80,000, left their beautiful Malibu, California, home. They had a fast-paced lifestyle that Jeff described as "running a 100-yard dash from Monday to Friday." They are now living in a small town making sheepskin mittens, vests and coats at a store they bought called The Sheepherder.

"Success used to mean graduation from college, getting out of the Army, getting a job, house, getting married, having kids—all the ordinary goals," Jeff reflected. "It then became more, more, more. None of it meant fulfillment. What really counts is being happy with your station in life and receiving contentment from your avocation and vocation."

Are you happy with your station in life? Do you have a feeling of contentment, or is there a stronger feeling that there must be more to life than you are experiencing? Are you tired of hearing about success, success, success, while feeling you haven't had your share? Do you enjoy reading the newspaper because it tells about people whose lives are in a worse mess than yours?

Success for some is how hard they work; for others it is how much they make without having to work very hard. My uncle Alvin Dreier, a farmer, once told me, "Some white-collar folks might think we are dumb because we have to work so hard for what we get."

My uncle's feelings were echoed by Gerald Wiens, who is head mechanic and supervisor for a fleet of school buses. "The way some people come across, wanting to work all the time isn't the right thing. If you work and enjoy your work, why not do it? It would drive me crazy to sit around and visit all day. I need to get out and turn a wrench. The curve in life is different for different people."

Have you ever felt less successful than someone else because you saw yourself working a lot harder to maintain the same lifestyle? I struggle with that at times. I will be working on a speech or an article and stop to think how many more hours I have to spend than others I know. Such comparisons are a waste of time and take away the energy for whatever I am doing. Nevertheless, these thoughts still go through my mind.

From my interviews I found that for many, success had taken on a new dimension and clarity since their lifestyle changes. I saw a definite shift from looking at success in terms of what mainstream society, TV ads and glossy magazines associate with it to looking at success from a more personal perspective.

For much of mainstream society, success has taken on a facade of power and money, quite a contrast to the success described by 27-year-old Elspeth Payne who works with the physically impaired. To her, success is helping a young girl learn to ski in a special tub—made for those who can't use their legs. "The look in the young girl's eyes makes it all worth while."

Success can create confusion in your plans if you do not differentiate between your version and the popularized version of success, although for some they may be the same. Admittedly, developing your own parameters of success is difficult when you are bombarded by literally thousands of inputs from ads trying to convince you to do and buy certain things to make you successful. But if you disregard your ideas because they don't represent success in society's eyes, you're putting your life on hold and you will be sorry.

Life isn't stagnant. Your values and your priorities are continually changing. Awareness of these subtle changes is important to living a life with greater harmony and fulfillment. Yesterday's yardsticks may no longer measure today's successes for you. What are some of the subtle changes that have taken place in what you consider important? How are these changes affecting your thinking about making a lifestyle change?

Making a lifestyle change is an attitude as much as an event. It is a flexible attitude that is focused on current needs and wants, not on outdated needs and wants. It is recognizing your uniqueness, and the uniqueness of your experiences and your life. It is allowing the events of today to help mold the direction of tomorrow. Today's events are the motivation for tomorrow's changes

WHY THEY CHANGED

Sixty-six in-depth interviews with those who made lifestyle changes created a mountain of experiences and feelings to assimilate. While there was a similarity of feelings among those interviewed, each person brought a unique perspective of how he/she had orchestrated change and how that change had led to a life of greater fulfillment.

People told of the circumstances, the feelings, the forces, the reasons that motivated them to make a change—many of which you may also be experiencing. As you will soon realize, there are a number of forces interacting on your life to keep you where you are now.

Circumstances arise—some in your control, some out of it—that push and pull your thinking. At a certain point, the pushing forces get so great, you decide to do something. You experience a whole new feeling and commitment to do more with your life. These circumstances may come on gradually, or they may happen all of a sudden. Some of the specific things that caused the interviewees to change were:

- got passed over for a job promotion
- father died an unexpected early death—I'm next
- felt I wasn't making any progress
- wanted to get away from suburban mentality
- wanted to have more time with husband
- was ready to meet some new friends
- was tired of business politics
- didn't want to rear children in suburbia
- was tired of the materialistic rat race
- wanted to rebuild marriage
- wanted to pursue my love of art
- was looking for other challenges
- sold company
- didn't want to wilt away in front of TV set
- was ready for something besides a plastic lifestyle
- didn't want to wait until retirement to enjoy life
- wanted to go beyond a pantyhose existence
- wanted to have more time with the kids
- was burned out

These feelings and circumstances were the "whacks on the side of the head" that helped us take our lives off hold. Most people need that gentle nudge or whack to get them to make a significant change. What kind of nudge or whack would it take for you?

LEARNING FROM OTHERS

Here is your opportunity to learn from others who have felt the same frustrations and urges you may be experiencing. It is through others' experiences that we get those emotional nudges that help us move off hold. Whether your lifestyle change is making an occupational change, a relationship change or a geographic/occupational change, I hope your transition will be made easier as you learn from those of us who have already walked through the door. You will also have an opportunity to hear what we have found on the other side of the door.

Our experiences will help you know where to look, what to expect and how to handle the uncertainties of change— much like formalized education opens your thinking to new horizons. What happens in your life is up to you.

Elspeth Payne had some advice for anyone who feels stuck: "It's just real important to think about what you like in life and why you are doing what you are doing. Are you happy or are you unhappy? Verbalize how you feel and get real honest with yourself. That helps me get moving."

Why are you doing what you are doing? Are you where you are by choice or are you stuck and don't know how to get moving? As you read the chapters that follow, let yourself open up to the feelings as well as the words of those sharing their experiences. Life's journey is easier as we learn from each other.

PSYCHOLOGICAL GHETTO

Have you ever surprised yourself by some of the things you have done that you never thought you could do? What's keeping you from doing them again? Do you feel fenced in?

As a Kansas farm boy, I was intrigued by how cows explored new fenced-in pastures. In the spring, Dad would turn the cows out to graze new, green wheat pastures. To keep the cows from roaming over the whole field at once, he would put up a temporary electric fence. It didn't take long for the cows to figure out right where the fence was. The curious ones would check out their boundaries by sniffing the shiny wire fence—and get an unexpected electric shock. From then on, they would stop before they came to the fence. After several days of grazing, you could see exactly where the fence was, for inside it the pasture was cropped very short while outside it was still lush and green.

When this area was grazed down, Dad would move the fence further back. The next morning they would come out to a larger field, but would only go to where the original fence had been. Eventually one of the more adventuresome cows would discover the fence had been moved, and the rest would follow.

In some ways, people are like cows. They try something, get a shock and avoid trying it again. They are afraid to risk going further. They are staying within the limits of the familiar, grazing it over and over and over. This becomes their psychological ghetto.

Unknowingly, you may be trapped by an invisible force—a psychological ghetto. It affects your thinking; it affects how you react to situations. You may not like it, you may find it frustrating, but it's familiar and gives you a feeling of security.

As is true with other ghettos, you will tend to surround yourself with others from the same ghetto—others with the same outlook and feelings. They in turn cause you to become more deeply entrenched in your ghetto.

Occasionally someone breaks out of the ghetto, leaving the rest behind. The breakaways are described as mavericks, strange, weird, filled with wanderlust. Or on a more positive note, they may be called entrepreneurs, self-starters, motivated or gutsy. Ultimately, others watching may also give it a try.

Do you feel as if you are caught in a ghetto? Are you ready to break through, or would you rather stay where you are? Are you stuck—you want to get out but you need a shot in the arm?

For some, like Ben, the shot in the arm has come from a good book or an inspiring motivational speaker. Ben told of how he was getting further and further in a rut. His girlfriend was threatening to break up with him if he didn't get his act together. "One evening, under my protest, she dragged me to hear Zig Ziglar speak. I am glad I went. He talked about all the people that stood around saying, 'It can't be done.' That was me. He had this old water pump and he was pumping away. He said, 'You work toward success a pump stroke at a time—so don't give up. Keep pumping.' That evening got me out of my rut."

What would it take to help you get out of your rut, your ghetto? Bob Hendrix, a psychotherapist, found, "Too often people come in and want me to 'fix it.' They want me to wave some magic wand. If a person wants to make a change, he has to take the responsibility for making the change. We usually want to put it off to some other person—mom, dad, the company or the government."

It's up to you to get out of the ghetto. Sherry, an energetic 31-year-old secretary, felt stuck. "I feel I have more potential than I am using," she said. Listening to Sherry talk, I also thought she wasn't using her full potential. Some of her potential was being wasted on complaining about how she felt she was being taken advantage of by others—boss, sister, boyfriend. Sherry's feelings had put her in a ghetto surrounded by walls of negativism.

Through the inspiration of a respected uncle, Sherry has started to crawl out of her ghetto. "He encouraged me to reach out to other people and not to be so wrapped up in protecting myself from others. I started by spending more time with the ladies at work. I was surprised as I reached out to them. Some of those I really hadn't cared for are becoming friendlier." Instead of focusing on people's faults, Sherry is now talking more about their good points.

Getting into a ghetto doesn't happen overnight, nor does getting out of it happen overnight. The boundaries have been formed over the years—especially in our early years. Input from parents, teachers and other adults helps form the boundaries of our ghetto.

"Our whole family has bad luck . . ." was the ghetto that Nancy, a high school senior, was already feeling. She told of hearing her parents and grandparents telling time and time again all the bad things that had happened to them. Now when anything bad happened, Nancy said she just felt that was the way it went for her family. She was afraid to think about college because she thought she would flunk out—just another bad thing for her family.

Do you ever get the feeling you were born on the wrong side of the tracks—that other families have it easier and are luckier than yours? If so, are you hanging on to that belief? Why? Is it working for you?

Unfortunately, people often don't realize they are clinging to mental attitudes that are not working for them. They may never take time to realize how their beliefs are affecting their lives. Faulty beliefs can keep you from breaking out of your ghetto, from reaching out for life.

"Birdy" was the nickname Clara got in grade school when the kids made fun of her long thin "bird legs." She had always been tall for her age and felt awkward towering over her classmates. "I often went home from high school crying thinking no boy would ever want to date me. When I was around other girls, I just knew the boys would rather talk to them than to me, so I would stand back. It was only after my mother kept cutting out magazine pictures of beautiful, tall girls that I started to be less shy and stand up straighter." When she changed her beliefs about herself, she changed her life.

What beliefs do you have about yourself that are keeping your life on hold? When was the last time someone suggested you try doing this or that and you replied, "I never could do that"? Why did you say that? Admittedly, in some cases special training or a special skill may be needed, but in other cases it's just a matter of having the belief in yourself.

I remember the time I was asked to teach Sunday school, and I said I couldn't because I was afraid to talk in front of people. After some coaxing I gave in. Now I enjoy it—and the butterflies even have left.

GHETTOS STIFLE THINKING

Our psychological ghettos stifle our thinking. They box us in, keeping us from seeing other options. An example of restrictive thinking was pointed out to me in a college psychology class. Perhaps you have seen the puzzle where you are asked to connect nine dots with four straight lines—they can cross each other but they can't overlap. Having done well in high school math and geometry, I figured this would be my chance to shine before my classmates.

I tried

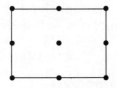

And I tried

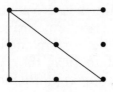

And I tried

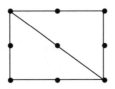

I didn't get it right, nor did anyone else in the class.

And finally I gave up. The right answer:

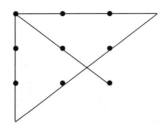

I failed to solve the problem because I worked within the confines of the nine dots. In my mind, I had put an invisible boundary around the nine dots. To solve the problem, I had to break past the invisible barrier I had set up.

That's also true of life. To accomplish our goals, we have to go beyond the imaginary boundaries—we have to break out of our box—we have to break out of our ghetto. Are you ready?

SELECTIVE LISTENING KEEPS YOU IN A GHETTO

If you were given a nice compliment by two different people and a third person said something negative about you, which would you remember the longest—the negative? If so, what does that tell you about your belief system and how you look at yourself? Most people tend to hear the negative more loudly—with the possible exception of politicians, who eventually become hardened to it.

Our selective hearing allows information to come through that is consistent with our beliefs about ourselves—the rest is sorted out. Gibbons, a 31-year-old lawyer, remarked, "I would remember the positive because I know I am a good person and even though they made a negative comment, if they really knew me, they wouldn't feel that way." His wife, Sarah, said, "I would probably dwell on the negative because I am afraid if they really knew me, they wouldn't have said the positive—of course it depends what the positive was. If they said I had a beautiful dress, I would accept that."

When someone compliments you, and, in your humility, you play down their compliment, you are in effect discrediting them in addition to not accepting your good news. Be willing to say "thank you" and breathe in the good feeling. When you receive a negative comment, evaluate it and, if it appears valid, be willing to make a change. This will help you start hearing things in a fresh way—a way to help you break out of your ghetto.

FRIENDS AND FAMILY CAN KEEP YOU IN A GHETTO

Your family and/or friends can help keep you in a ghetto. Through their caring and concern for you, they may say or do things that could hold you back if you aren't careful.

I remember my feelings when I decided to go into the seminar business back in 1971. I phoned my folks in Kansas to tell them of my plans. My dad, who was a plant manager for a manufacturing company in Hesston, responded by saying, "I get dozens of brochures coming across my desk every day telling about all kinds of seminars. It looks to me like that's going to be a darn hard way to make a living. . ." and at first it was. While Dad's response sounded negative, I later realized he spoke out of concern that I wasn't just going into something blindly.

The first 10 months were financially scary as I called on businesses and heard "no" over and over again; "After you have a track record we might be interested in talking to you"; "We don't have money in our budget right now." If it hadn't been for Karen, who was giving piano lessons to up to 35 students a week, we would have had to borrow money for groceries.

In the 10th month my mother showed her concern about how slow things were going for me. "Maybe you should consider trying to get a real job." While it hurt to hear that, I knew she was saying it from a position of caring.

Comments such as these can momentarily cause us to slide back into our old ways of doing things—back to the familiar. It would have been easy for me to do, for while I wanted to be in business for myself, there was a feeling of security when working for someone else and getting a regular paycheck.

When Charles and Sally told their friends of their plans to make a lifestyle change which would take them to another state, they found, "Our friends actually got mad at us for leaving. They accused us of running away from them and not really caring about their feelings. That was seven years ago, and now most of them have also moved. We are glad we didn't let them hold us back."

When Scott Graysmith, an acupuncturist, and his wife, Nancy, decided to leave the high-speed life of Chicago, some of Scott's patients became very upset about his leaving. Nancy noted, "Some friends didn't believe we would actually move. When we told them, they just patted us on the head and said 'Oh, sure!'"

If you make a lifestyle change that includes a move, be ready for comments from those who care about you. While you may feel they are trying to run your life, realize that they hate to see you go.

What are you afraid your family or friends might say that would hold you back? How will you respond?

BREAKING OUT OF THE GHETTO
WITH A GEOGRAPHIC MOVE

A geographic move is the impetus needed for some people to get out of the ghetto. Larry, a 30-year-old teacher, said, "I finally got on my own two feet when I moved away from my home community. I met new people with new ways of thinking. All my family had grown up in the same basic area and we all thought most of the U.S. was like we had it. I discovered it's different." In his home community, everyone knew Larry as the math teacher's kid—his dad was the math teacher at the small local high school. "I now feel I have more of my own identity," Larry said after his move. "I have started doing more creative thinking about what I want to do with my life. Maybe some people can shine in their home community; I needed to get away."

My experience was similar. I have always felt that after leaving my home community, I took some risks and did some things I wouldn't have tried before. Yet I love going back home to the familiar rural area and hearing my old nickname, "Muscles," called out.

Yolanda told of growing up in a very close family. "As I grew older, I found myself coasting and not taking responsibility for my own life. Even at the age of 40, when I had a problem, I would turn to my folks. This was very frustrating to my husband. I needed to get away."

After she and her husband moved, "It forced me to rely on my own thinking more. I went out and applied for a job in a big company. If you would have told me eight months ago I would be doing what I am doing now, I would have never believed you. I feel so much better about myself than I used to. The move broke me out of a rut."

Do you feel your thinking is restricted where you are living right now, or does the security of where you are help build personal confidence? For some, a geographic move takes away their base. How would your life be different if you made a move? What might you try that you aren't willing to try now?

You don't necessarily have to make a geographic move to break out of a rut, but you do have to take some kind of action. The longer your life is on hold, the deeper you get entrenched in your ghetto.

NOT LIVING IN THE NOW
KEEPS YOU IN THE GHETTO

Are you present in the present? As you read right now, are you here or has your mind wandered off someplace else and you find yourself having to go back and reread what you just read? That also happens to me. It is very easy to get caught in a trap thinking about the future or rehashing the past while the present goes slipping by.

Judy, an executive secretary whom I have counseled, is caught in a ghetto of always looking back. She has a continual string of regrets: "I should have spent more time with my kids. I should have waited to get married. I shouldn't have bought that last car. I should have gotten a college degree." Her life can be pictured as someone walking backward. She doesn't see the now moments until she walks past them. Do you ever find yourself doing that?

Then there is the other extreme with Ronna, a computer programmer. "I fret and stew over the future, will this happen, will that happen, and by the time it gets here I am tired of it. Someone can be talking to me and I don't hear them. I'm off thinking about something else. It has created some serious problems in our marriage."

As Jane Hendrix, a psychotherapist, pointed out, "Not living in the present is a form of denial. It's easier to live in the past or future because then I don't have to be responsible for the present, and, in so doing, I deny any feelings associated with the present."

This denial was experienced by Carolyn Lohman, who was not aware of how emotionally out of touch she was with the now moments until coming down with an illness that could have been terminal. "It was then I realized that I have spent most of my life not living in the now. It is fairly common to find people, particularly in the city, going about doing the things they think they need to do or that they feel they should do—they miss a very important part of their life—I did."

Listen to yourself talk. Are you living in the present, past or future? Do you think about what you are experiencing at the moment—the beautiful sunset, the nice music, friends, health, disappointments—or are you numb to the present?

The present has many inputs that can help you break out of your ghetto. When you are present in the present, your mental energy is focused on maximizing the present. You are more aware of the opportunities you now have, which in turn affect your future course. There is nothing wrong with thinking and planning for the future and learning from the past, except when you do it at the expense of the beauty of the moment.

GOAL MINING

FROM WHAT TO WHAT

In researching this book, I found a surprising number of people who said they would like to make a lifestyle change, but to what??? They felt confused and frustrated not knowing how to decide what they really wanted. You might say they were mining for goals—digging, searching, but not sure for what.

"One of the difficulties I have is I don't know what I would like to change to . . . ," was the frustration felt by Ina Bartel, 55, a personnel assistant. "I don't know what would be the most wonderful thing in the world to do. I don't have a clear picture of what utopia is like."

What would be utopia for you? Would it be confusing and frustrating to try to decide? Would you feel like a child walking into a big candy store and being told to pick out your favorite candy? Would that be mind-boggling?

You have many opportunities if you are willing to reach out for them. It's your choice. It's more than making a change for the sake of change; rather, it's making a change for greater fulfillment and harmony in your life.

In making a change, you may be committing to a new job, a new relationship, a new way of life. An important question for consideration: Is your commitment to the *activity* of change or to the *results* of change? There is a big difference. It is easy to confuse activity with results.

An analogy would be the sport of fishing. My parents love the excitement of waiting for the cork to bob. I much prefer catching to fishing—and I also prefer catching to cleaning.

After awhile, I get bored if no fish are caught. The activity is fishing; the results are catching.

As a 10-year-old, I had to practice the piano for 30 minutes every day. Remember those days? I went through that activity on a daily basis, but, after hundreds of dollars worth of piano lessons, I can just barely play a few simple hymns. The activity was there, but the results weren't.

The same is often true of people's lives. They focus on the activity of their lives, not on the results. Making a lifestyle change is an activity that is aimed at certain results. The results are the fruits of your activities. What do you want to see different as the result of taking your life off hold? In what ways are you caught up in the activity of living, rather than in the results of living?

Some people's lives might be compared to driving a car; they have their foot on the gas pedal, but they don't know where they are going. As they watch the scenery whiz by, they may think they are making real progress, while in fact they are just going in a big circle.

When you have goals in your life, you avoid going in a circle. Your challenge is to decide what goals you want to see satisfied as a result of taking your life off hold.

On one hand it is exciting to wildly fantasize about all the options available to you. On the other hand, it is confusing and threatening if you haven't done it before. Normally people take life in a more structured vein. When your mind is let out of its cage, sometimes there is the fear it might get out of control. It won't. Allow it to be. It is all a process of deciding where you want to goal mine. Goal mining begins with dreaming.

DISCOVERY THROUGH DREAMING

Contrary to what your parents told you, it's okay to daydream. I remember watching our two sons stare into space as they sat in front of their homework. My comment to them was, "Don't waste your time daydreaming"—that's what my folks always told me. While there is a time and place for daydreaming, it is not a waste of time.

The challenges of everyday living often do not leave much time for dreaming. Rather, it is often a matter of keeping on keeping on. Our energy is absorbed by trying to keep our heads above water. After months and years of this intense lifestyle, our ability to dream becomes like a muscle that hasn't been used—it gets weak.

"People who are achievement oriented function a lot with their parent and adult ego state,"said psychotherapist Bob Hendrix. "When you ask someone what they want, their thinking goes into their child ego state, which has the ability to fantasize. Those who have spent more of their time in the parent and adult ego states are often afraid of their child ego state because they think it will go hog-wild and dog crazy—and they won't give themselves permission to do that. You ask a child what they want and they can tell you right away. You ask an adult and they often don't know."

Children are masters at dreaming. Their dreaming keeps their imaginations running overtime. How many of you parents have bought your children a $25 toy that you couldn't wait until they opened the box. Thirty minutes later, the toy sat in the corner while they played with the box it came in. As you watched, you discovered the box was now a monster, a big truck or whatever else they decided to make it. Their imaginations allowed that box to be whatever they decided.

Take a lesson from children. Exercise your imagination—exercise your right brain. Pick up a glass and think of five ways that glass is like your life. Think of the ways a chair is like your life. Look at a wallpaper design and think of what lessons it can teach you about life.

Doing what you just did exercises your right brain. Yes, you have two brains—a right and a left. Jacquelyn Wonder, co-author of *Whole Brain Thinking*, found that the right brain does the creative daydreaming while the left brain is for more routine day-to-day activities. "By practicing daydreaming, followed by visualization, you will be better able to solve problems and plan strategies for your life."

Without question, the mind has much more power than is ever used. In tapping just a portion of that potential, you will uncover new answers to past confusions.

While you may feel confused about the next step in your life, the information is in your subconscious mind. The challenge is to get it to your conscious mind. This takes opening up the doors of your thinking. Your subconscious mind is gently knocking at the door of your conscious mind. Unfortunately, with the emotional noise of everyday living, the knock is often not heard. Therefore, you need to look behind every door— exercising your mind helps do that.

TAKING YOUR DAYDREAMING ONE STEP FURTHER

In gold mining, we think of staking out claims—likewise in goal mining. In gold mining, the claim is staked out where the prospector feels there is the most gold. Then he starts digging. In goal mining, you may be uncertain where you would like to stake a claim. You feel confused and frustrated. But a little preliminary probing will help you decide on your options.

It would be nice if we could turn on our home video machine to see ourselves in different situations, and then decide which we liked best. While we can't at this stage of technological development, we can use our minds to come close to it through the process of visualization.

Visualization goes one step beyond the free-floating daydreaming mentioned earlier. In visualization you direct what you are seeing in your mind's eye. You are the director and the main character. You decide where the scene is going to take place, the time of day, what you are wearing, who else is present, and the final outcome of your mental movie.

Visualization breaks us out of the predictable mold that we have settled in. You probably know people who before they open their mouths, you know what they are going to say. You know how they are going to react, you know their walk, their way of laughing. We all fall into patterns of behavior that keep our thinking on hold.

Visualization stretches your thinking. If you are a serious person, close your eyes and pretend you are at a party laughing, joking, doing things in complete contrast to your normal way.

If you have a fear of talking to strangers, see yourself walking up and confidently talking to a stranger.

Some people feel they can't expect more than they have right now. They feel they don't deserve it. They find that when they visualize great things in their lives, they are brought back to a reality that says you have all you are going to get.

Are you able to let your mind flow or do you feel you can't have or don't deserve more? If others can have it, why can't you? What makes them more special than you?

Visualization can have an impact on your business as well as on your personal life. Eric Greenhut, a 50-year-old retired wholesale distributor, told how he visualized retiring at age 50. "In running my company, I had a vision of employees taking more and more of the responsibility. As the employees became more competent, I had more time to sit back and visualize what I would like to do upon retirement. When I sold the company, I had mentally prepared myself for the change and knew what I wanted to do—didn't just jump from owner to retiree." Today Eric and his wife enjoy six months on a sailboat in Florida and the other six months in the mountains.

Teresa Bressert told how important visualization had been to her and her husband, Walter, in making their lifestyle change. "In making our change, we visualized the type of lifestyle we wanted. One that would use our creative powers in a more relaxed setting. Our vision came true. Our visualization helped us plan."

While I have found visualization to be a powerful tool that helps me unravel my thinking as I first visualize one option, then another, I have met others who are very skeptical of the whole process—like Raymond.

Raymond had been fired from his position as president of a medium-sized company. Devastated and confused, he came to me asking for advice. When I suggested he spend some quiet time visualizing different options, his comeback was, "I have spent the past 17 years watching balance sheets, dealing with union problems, fighting the government. That is the real world to me. For me to spend time doing that visualizing doesn't make any sense. That is not the real world. My decisions are based on numbers, not dreams."

Raymond is a strong left-brained person—very analytical. His thinking is rigid. In trying to explore other options, he needs to get his right brain involved, to do some dreaming. He needs to stretch outside the traditional boundaries of his thinking. By being so analytical, he is limiting the power of his mind. It would be like tying your right arm behind your back and trying to function. You could do it, but it would be slower and there would be some things that you couldn't do—such as clapping your hands.

Through visualization, you can mentally try things on for size. As you visualize different episodes, pay attention to how your stomach feels. How does your neck feel? Is your breathing changing? All these are subtle indicators of liking or disliking what is being visualized.

After selling my business in Dallas, I wasn't sure what I wanted to do next. The business sale had taken place during a six-week period, with most of the time spent on working out details. This hadn't left much time for detailed planning.

There were questions that needed to be answered. In sorting out my thinking, I sat in the backyard and visualized what it would be like to move away from our home in Irving, a Dallas suburb. What would it be like to open another office and start over again? What would it be like to take off time to write a book? What would it be like to just give seminars and not get into another business where other employees were needed?

During this visualization, my heart and body were continually reacting to what I was thinking. I found that my heart rate would speed up when I was thinking about tense business situations. I felt calm when thinking about continuing to give talks and starting to write a book. My body was reacting to the situation I was visualizing. Some of the reactions were surprising. It was as if my body had information, through the subconscious mind, that I wasn't consciously aware of. And in fact, that is often the case.

Because the subconscious mind holds all we have ever heard, said or read, it does have access to feelings and information that we are unaware of. In your state of confusion about not knowing what you want to do in the next chapter of your life, your subconscious mind has the information to help you make this important decision. One way of listening to our subconscious mind is by observing our body's reactions.

In my seminars I ask people to shut their eyes and imagine going to their kitchen refrigerator and taking out a lemon. They take the lemon over to the kitchen counter, cut it in half and smell it. As I observe their facial reactions, it is as if they had bitten into a real lemon. They tell how saliva starts flowing in their mouths. The subconscious can't tell the difference between a real lemon and a vividly imagined lemon.

As you visualize in detail different possibilities for your life, your subconscious will think the event is actually taking place and your body will respond accordingly. There will be good feelings and tense feelings spread through your body giving you clues to what ideas are in harmony or out of harmony with your values and personality.

As you try to decide where you want to stake your claim in this goal mining process, visualization can help you probe to see what is under the surface. It helps take away some of the risk of blindly digging in the dirt hoping by chance to find a valuable goal.

WRITING OUT YOUR FUTURE

If you were to write down what you would like to see happen in the rest of your life, what would you say? Does the very thought of doing that scare you—or does it sound like fun? Doing it might be compared to developing a prospector's map for gold mining.

Early in my business career, I attended a seminar on life planning. One of the activities to help us set a direction in our lives was to write out our autobiographies the way we wanted them to look when we were 85. At the time I was 31, and 85 seemed a long way off. We were told to let our imaginations run wild and not deny ourselves anything that we wanted.

I went to a nearby lake and sat down on a log. I sat and I sat, but nothing came forth. I was stuck. I wasn't used to this kind of fantasizing. When I would think of something, I was reluctant to write it down because I wasn't sure if that was what I really wanted. Or I may have wanted it but felt silly putting it down because I didn't think I could ever have it. As you can see, I was using a very analytical, left-brain approach.

Eventually, the thought of the embarrassment of going back to the seminar room with a blank piece of paper got me started writing at least something. I began by thinking of all the possessions I would like to have—a Mercedes, a house with a swimming pool, a boat. Then came the thought of having my own business, being a public speaker in all 50 states, going on trips overseas with my family. When the hour was up, I had filled several pages from my yellow pad.

When I got home, I took those pages and hid them behind my socks in a dresser drawer. One Sunday afternoon several months later, I got them out and read them again. What I had written still seemed farfetched, but interesting. Every three to six months I would dig those pages out and look at them again. Each time, my ideas seemed a little more possible. Seventeen years later, they had all come true—and I am not 85 yet. What seemed like a questionable activity 17 years ago now has special meaning to me.

What I understand now—that I didn't understand then—is that during the process of writing my autobiography, I was stretching my thinking and planting seeds in my subconscious mind. The seeds became goals which I began to work toward systematically.

Writing your autobiography the way you want it to look when you are 85 is an approach to help you break out of a rut in your thinking. Just like the miners found when digging for gold, there are a variety of approaches that can be used when directing your thinking to help set lifestyle goals.

REAL GOLD OR FOOL'S GOLD

How do you know if you have real gold or fool's gold is a question often asked by novice gold miners. A similar question is asked by goal miners—such as Lorene. "My fear is that I will commit my life to some goal and when I get it, it won't be worth the effort."

Have you ever saved and saved for something and when you finally got it you were disappointed? It's even more disappointing when you trade years of your life for a goal that ends up not meeting your expectations.

Such was the case of Hank, who worked at a manufacturing company for 29 years, counting the days until he could retire. "I hated going to work but I didn't want to give up my retirement benefits. The older I got the harder it was to think about switching companies. The only thing that kept me going was the thought of retiring. Now that I am retired, I'm bored. I feel lost. I hate to think of all the years I plowed through just waiting for this day."Have you ever met anyone who felt this way? If so, what did you learn from what he/she had to say?

Knowing what goals will stand the test of time is a serious concern. To get a fresh perspective, I spoke with people who have grappled with sorting out real gold from fool's gold, the significant from the insignificant, the important from the unimportant. Valuable nuggets can be gained from the elderly— those with a longer historical perspective—such as my parents.

My 74-year-old parents have gone through several sobering experiences during their lives. Each time they took stock of life's bottom line. Dad had rheumatic fever at age 16, leaving him with a bad heart; three days after my folks were married, Dad's mother died; their first child died three days after birth. In their early 40s, they had to sell the farm because of financial pressures, and Dad went to work at a local factory. More recently, my dad had two heart valves replaced in open-heart surgery.

My dad's opinion of what's important in life? "You need to make your life worthwhile. Do some kind of service to humanity."Since his retirement 10 years ago, he has been volunteering at a psychiatric hospital in Newton, Kansas.

Dad's advice to those considering a lifestyle change is,"They had better make some solid plans to do something they feel is worthwhile that is going to contribute to their life instead of just spending their time fishing or taking trips. If they don't, their life isn't going to last very long."

In reflecting back over her life, my mother stressed the importance of being sensitive to other people and their thinking. "You have to work at doing what is right—not only what you want to do, but what is the right thing."She also spoke of the importance of stretching oneself. "Be interested in learning and reaching out and accepting challenges. Do things even if you are scared."

Bernice Anderson, 92, has been an inspiration to me ever since I met her in Malawi, Central Africa. She is an author, composer of two children's operettas, a woman who, with her husband, made a major lifestyle change in her late 60s and went to Africa to work with the Cooperative Development Program. Her secret is to, "Just try to live up to the quote from *Hamlet*, Act I, 'to thine own self be true, and it must follow, as the night the day, thou canst not then be false to any man.'"

Bernice has been true to a life filled with continual exploring, always reaching out to others. At age 85, she had her latest book published and began touring the United States to autograph copies of it. At 92, she is still writing articles and poems for publication.

Vivienne Bodeau, 72, saw many sides of life as she traveled around the world as a war correspondent for various newspapers and magazines. She shared with me how she had worked with a number of presidents and knew them quite well. She saw politics at work, she saw the horrors of war firsthand, she attended "plastic" government and embassy social gatherings. Vivienne still keeps very busy with community and senior affairs and a weekly newspaper column. What would this intrepid woman say to someone who was scared to make a lifestyle change? "I don't think there's ever a percentage in being scared whether you are in a war zone or making a change in your life. You have to make a decision and stick with it. You can't vacillate."

When asked about quality living, she replied, "Many people are interested in money and stay interested in it, taking it to the grave with them. And really they have missed so much. You have to take time to watch a bird fly, or see a tree grow, or time to think. Some slow down after a traumatic illness, but then it's a little too late. There is a quality of life that is terribly important and you'll never repeat this life, so if you don't do it now, you never will."

"Go for it!"is a message repeated over and over by the elderly. But when you go for it, don't forget others in your life.

What is your philosophy on what makes a fulfilling life? Are you taking your own advice or are you just paying lip service to what sounds good?

Another source of valuable insight comes from the terminally ill. They have a closeness to the basics of life that is often overlooked during normal high-speed living. In their fear and pain, the terminally ill see life from a perspective uncluttered by social pressures and man-made frills. Instead, they see the essence of life.

Allen Nesbitt, a Methodist minister and counselor, told of the soul-searching people go through as they learn of their serious illness. "You can't imagine how quickly some people's values shift when they are threatened with death. They suddenly take a new look at what is important in life."

At the death of a family member or friend, we may take another look at our own lives. Such was the case with my wife's uncle Virgil Flickenger's untimely death from cancer. Virgil's death made me aware of the importance of not putting things off until tomorrow—whether it is doing something or telling others that you love them.

During his last week, he called his four children into his room one by one and talked to them in a way that few children experience from a dad. There was a quality to those moments that his children will never forget. They saw how their dad had feelings, concerns and dreams for them that had never been expressed with such emotion.

Have you ever wondered what the dead would tell us about life if they could talk? I have. After Grandma Dreier's funeral, I spent some time strolling through the small country graveyard. Many of the people buried there I had known.

I remember Uncle Johnny who was known for his big farm, Lawrence Molzen who was always running as he built houses, Aunt Mamie who was always dressed so neatly. Walking by the gravestones, I thought of the disappointments, the frustrations, the financial concerns, the prestige concerns that each of these people undoubtedly felt in their lives. Now none of it mattered. If these people could talk, I wondered what advice they would give about living a full life? What would they hold up as being the important values of life?

THE NEED FOR PURPOSE

Regardless of the type of lifestyle change you make, you need purpose to enjoy it. Have you ever felt it would be great to do nothing day after day? It's not. It's boring.

George Snow, 39, gave up a lucrative sales position to enjoy a new lifestyle of leisure. He had this to say about his change: "I used to hate doing all the paperwork in sales. I couldn't wait until I had enough money to just do nothing for a while. The first two months after quitting my job I loved it—getting up late, playing golf, going fishing, lots of reading. By the third month my balloon was going down. Instead of feeling happy, I felt worthless.

"I had to have something to do, so I started doing volunteer work, which I now really enjoy. I have my own time schedule, it doesn't have a lot of pressure and I am doing something worthwhile. People are crazy if they think that the pot of gold at the end of the rainbow is to just play."

Agreed! There is more to life than watching the TV soaps and doing leg lifts. You need purpose, a sense of direction. Working toward meaningful goals brings excitement to your life. Goals can help you to become more self-disciplined. If you are used to being in a structured situation with set hours and set policies, it is easy to get sidetracked when you make a lifestyle change to less structure. I have found this especially true while writing this book. When I look out and see those beautiful snow-covered mountains, it is tempting to take the day off and go skiing, but that doesn't get the next chapter written.

If you are frustrated because you can't decide on any particular goals, have patience and keep goal mining—keep digging. The more clearly you have your goals defined, the happier you will be with your change. You may find that after you make your change, you may add new goals or change some of the old ones. That is all right. Goals are not etched in stone. They are guidelines to help focus your attention.

OVERCOMING PROCRASTINATION

Now that you have given thought to your goal mining, the next step is to start the actual digging. Many people think about goals and making a lifestyle change and stop there. As a friend, Sherill, asked, "Will your book tell how and where I can get the motivation to actually do something about my situation? This would be especially valuable for us that have procrastination down to a fine science."

If you are one of those who is a talker rather than a doer, a key question for you to consider is, "What's it going to be like when I don't have the energy and health that I now have, and I look back thinking, 'Why didn't I . . . ?'" Who are you going to blame for your being stuck? Who are you going to blame for your life having been on hold? In Aunt Joan's words, "Today is not tomorrow—do it now."

The importance of doing it now was expressed by psychotherapist Jane Hendrix. Both Jane and her husband, Bob, have slowed down and are taking more time to do things they always wanted to do. Jane explained what prompted this change: "Bob's mother was diagnosed as having cancer. All the old people were dying and we were next up. It's as if with someone else's dying you don't know how long you are going to live. The fragility and fleetingness of life became apparent, so I decided that if we were ever going to do it, we were going to do it now."

A full life takes action. It takes a belief that there is more and that it's worth going for. It's recognizing that you can do something about taking your life off hold.

TOOLS FOR GOAL MINING

The following activities and questions are designed to help you by giving step-by-step directions to goal-mining tools mentioned in this chapter. Goals are a significant part of the road map you use to chart a lifestyle change.

How to Visualize

If you are not familiar with visualization, the following may seem awkward at first, but will become very rewarding with repetition. Some people worry because they don't see a mental picture when they close their eyes. It is not absolutely necessary to mentally see an image. The mental image may be replaced with just thinking about what you are trying to visualize. Allow 5 to 15 minutes for visualizing.

1. Find a place that is quiet and where you won't be disturbed by the phone or someone walking by.

2. Take several deep breaths. Each time you exhale, breathe out any tension that you are holding. Get yourself in a relaxed state so your mind is free and fluid.

3. Create a movie screen in your mind and see the images you want to visualize being shown on the screen.

4. Move from the parts you see to the parts you still want to see. Allow your mind to flow. If it wanders off the mental picture, be aware of where it is wandering. Is it headed toward fearful or exciting situations? Now move back to your guided visualization.

5. Put the mental picture in context. If it is a place you might want to move, see yourself there smelling the fresh air. Look at the sky and other scenery. See yourself making the move. Feel the excitement. See others responding to your change.

6. Visualize something really different that you would like to experience. Maybe you would like to be a movie star or an Olympic Gold Medal athlete. Maybe you would like to go on a month-long cruise. Enjoy the power of visualization as your mind takes you any place you want to go.

7. As you visualize, pay attention to how you feel inside. What tenses you up? What excites you? Your visualization can help you test the waters of making a variety of lifestyle changes. Over a period of days, see which images feel the best to you. You then can start exploring those ideas more seriously.

A Tool to Help You Determine
What You Really Want

If you still are frustrated about not knowing what you really want to do and what goals you want to set, let old magazines help you.

Take a magazine with a lot of pictures in it. As you page through the magazine, tear out those advertisements and pictures that give you a good feeling. You may not know initially why you have the good feeling. It is not important to know at this time. You may find a picture that shows a happy family around a table, or a picture that shows a confident person walking down the street, or a view that captures your interest.

The pictures you select tell about some of your internal needs and wants. With all the pictures in front of you, look at each picture and go into detail about why you like it. You may find a theme running through the pictures that wasn't obvious to you at first.

You will discover what feelings, what views, what values are important to you. This gives you a springboard from which to work as you set goals. It is important that your goals take into account what you have learned from this exercise.

The Mechanics of Setting Goals
Taking into account what you have discovered from the magazines and other ideas in this chapter, you can now start to get more specific with your goals. Goals have two major parts—a specific result that can be measured —and a definite time of desired completion.

If your goal is to be a happier person, that's not specific enough. Rather, ask what specific changes you would notice about yourself if you were happier. Would you be able to sleep better? Would you have fewer frown marks on your face? Would your blood pressure be lower? Would you laugh more? All these things can actually be measured or observed.

When do you want to complete your goal? In writing this book, I had a certain date I wanted to complete the interviewing, a timetable for each chapter and a completion date for the entire manuscript. These goals helped me keep on target.

If you are confused about what goals you want to set, your first step may be to set a deadline for establishing those goals. Let's imagine you want to have clarified your thinking on your lifestyle goal in three months. Between now and then you may set some minor steps to help you reach the main goal. For example, in the first month you may want to come up with eight different options. In the second month you talk to people who have the type of lifestyle you are exploring. In the third month you narrow your choices to three and explore each of them in more depth.

After deciding what you want to do, your next major goal will be to set a timetable for planning the details and making your change. The rest of this book will help you in working through the details and the emotions of change.

THE FORCES OF CHANGE

Rarely do people take time to explore the many personal forces affecting their lives. Your life's direction is the result of a set of forces. The better you understand the forces pushing and pulling at your life, the more control you will have over your destiny and the better you will be able to untangle the complex mental web that may be keeping you stuck.

One of the things I remember from a high school physics class is that a body will remain at rest until acted upon by a force. A ball resting on a table will not move until someone gives it a nudge. We won't move either until we get a nudge. Our nudge may be mental or physical. It may be the gentle nudge of a dream we would like to pursue—or the whack of getting fired from a job. It may be the frustration of a deteriorating relationship or unexpected health problems.

Sometimes we are kept on hold by stronger forces that oppose the nudge to move forward. The opposing forces may stem from a lack of confidence, fears of uncertainty, financial concerns, family concerns. These may be valid reasons or excuses.

What nudges do you feel pushing you toward change? What excuses are you making for not changing? Although you may believe your reasons are not excuses, let's assume they are for now, for the purpose of helping you break loose.

More than half of those interviewed admitted they hadn't made lifestyle changes earlier because of excuses they had allowed to guide their thinking. As retired salesman John Ray said, "It's sometimes difficult to distinguish the difference between a real consideration and an excuse. We always feel we have a good reason for doing or not doing something."

To break out of a rut, new ways of looking at things need to be explored. At first glance, the new way may not seem to fit, but if you give it a chance, you will gain new insight. Stubborn thinking keeps you stuck. You probably know people who, regardless of what you suggest, always have a reason it won't work for them. Don't be one of them.

There are thinkers and there are doers. The thinkers keep themselves busy thinking and never really make any changes. Sometimes they would like to change but don't know how to get started. They become so frustrated that they chuck the notion and settle back in the old rut.

John Ray felt this frustration. "Every time I think about doing something new, I get tense, my heart starts racing, my hands get sweaty, so I stay where I am. I guess I'm one of those who has gotten in a rut so deep, I'm afraid to get out of it. It has become a secure world for me."

John's feelings echo those of others. While they think about making changes, they don't act. Instead, they stick with Monday Night Football, bridge and bi-weekly golf outings.

When people talk about change, they talk about what they would like to do. Too often this is followed by why they can't do it and why they are going to stay where they are. There are forces pushing them toward change and forces holding them back. The strongest forces win—so there's either forward movement or things remain status quo.

"I wish I had the guts you have," was a common reaction that I got when making my lifestyle change. This was followed by people telling me how they would really like to make a change. When asked why they didn't, they gave me a whole list of reasons:

"I can't afford it."
"We've finally made the house the way we want it."
"Hate to leave our friends."
"I've worked so long to get where I am—
     I hate to start over."
"The kids."
"My spouse."

People like Carol were frustrated. A high school math teacher, Carol wanted to make a change but was resisting. Although she was reading every new self-help book she could find, she still felt stuck. "After carefully looking at the forces that were pushing me to change and those opposing change, I understood why I was still stuck. I had a lot more opposing forces than I ever realized. It took some serious soul-searching to see why I was holding on to some of those forces. I guess I was just scared. There seemed to be so much uncertainty and risk in change. It has helped me to make lists of these forces of uncertainty and work with them."

Imagine having a car that you think isn't going as fast as it could. A mechanic tells you that you have two problems: the brakes are dragging and the motor needs to be tuned.

Because of the cost, you try to decide if you can get by just taking care of one of the problems. You're in a quandary. If you tune up the motor and the brakes are still dragging, you won't get the full speed out of the car. What you have done is worked on the pushing force, but not on the force holding the car back.

Likewise, if you work on the brakes, but the motor still needs tuning, you won't get full potential from the car. Life is the same way. If your brakes are a dragging, opposing force or if your engine lacks motivation, you won't experience your full potential. Both forces need to be considered—the pushing and the opposing.

When I got ready to make my lifestyle change, there were a number of pushing and opposing forces to consider.

After writing down all the forces, a numerical value was assigned to each force. I gave the most important force on the diagram a value of 10 and the least important a value of one. Based on those two extremes, the remaining forces were assigned values between one and 10.

PUSHING FORCES			OPPOSING FORCES
want to live where scenery is more beautiful	5 >	< 4	still have two sons in college
want to get out of the rat race	7 >	< 5	boys may miss home place
tired of keeping up big place	6 >	< 8	we may regret selling all our things
want to reduce cost of living	7 >	< 5	we may not survive financially
want to write in a relaxed setting	10 >	< 3	it may be a mistake to put my business experience on hold at age 48
want to meet new people	6 >		
want to experience new life-style while still have health	6 >	< 1	giving up roots in the community
can move into our Breckenridge condo	5 >	< 6	will miss friends
	52 Total	32 Total	

When I added all the pushing forces, the total was 52. The total of the opposing forces was 32. Because the total of the pushing forces was greater than the opposing, I made the change.

At the end of this chapter, there is a diagram for you to analyze some of the forces affecting a change you have been contemplating. You may find that you give more than one force a value of 10 or a value of one. One side may have more forces than the other.

You may be surprised at what you find. If you find that the total of the pushing forces is greater, yet you are not making a change, then you have either inaccurately assessed the values for the forces in your diagram, or you have overlooked some opposing forces. One retarding force—fear—is discussed in detail later in this chapter. Fear tends to amplify the significance of most retarding forces. Fear adds a strong emotional element to uncertainties and concerns.

For some, frustration with the current situation is one of the main pushing forces. As frustration increases, a change will occur. For example, a person may begin with a frustrated feeling. That frustration may cause the person to feel unappreciated. As the feeling of being stuck becomes more pronounced, the pushing forces start increasing little by little.

Such was the case with Tom Joslin, 48, who worked many years for the federal government with the intention of eventually retiring. A high level of frustration forced him to re-examine his situation.

"I decided to change because I was burned out with the system. I had been working for the federal government 25 years, going through the ranks. I had gotten to a good position and was passed over for a job. The bureaucracy finally beat me down. I realized I couldn't go any further in the racket and play those games, the politicking, don't-make-waves mentality. It was grinding me down —thank God I am still not there!

"When I started talking about leaving my job and going into teaching, my family and I all sat down around the kitchen table and counted our pennies. The whole family agreed, `Hey! Go for it.' Our main consideration was if Dad stops making the lion's share of the money, what does this do to our lifestyle? I had another job in the wings so it wasn't like I was stepping off into an abyss. It basically revolved around lifestyle, with teenagers asking what happens if I didn't bring home the amount of money we had all gotten used to. My wife was very supportive. She is a schoolteacher—but we can't live off her salary.

"I took a 50 percent cut in pay. Would I do it again? Gosh, yes, without a question. Timing was perfect. The right place, the right time, a job waiting. I feel God was there—He had to be. If the job offer had come along a couple years earlier, I would have had to count my pennies a lot closer. I couldn't have helped my kids through college.

"Life is so much more meaningful to me now. I look forward to going to work each day. I don't get as snippy with my loved ones. The pressure is off me. I sent a letter to some of my out-of-state friends and told them it has taken wrinkles off my 48-year-old face, and it seems that I am sprouting new hair on my graying head. I would recommend that anyone in a dead-end situation should seriously look around. Life is too short to stay in a job you don't like. There are other possibilities if you just open up your thinking."

When Tom evaluated some of the forces that came into play when deciding to leave his job and go into teaching, it looked like this:

PUSHING FORCES		OPPOSING FORCES
frustration from being passed over for a job	>	< unable to create change
		< take 50% cut in pay
feel unappreciated	>	< give up 25 years of seniority
tired of politicking	>	< cut back on lifestyle
have another job offer	>	< kid coming up for college
feel burned out	>	< may not like teaching
want less tension	>	

Why did Tom wait so long to make his move? Going back just two years, some of the major forces involved were:

PUSHING FORCE		OPPOSING FORCES
tired of politicking	>	< not sure where would go
want less tension	>	< need money for college kids
		< like current lifestyle
		< have security at current job
		< opportunity for advancement

In this second diagram Tom had hope for job advancement. He was concerned about providing a good lifestyle for his family, including his kids in college. While this is still a concern for his younger daughter, who will soon graduate from high school, it assumed a lower priority when Tom was passed over for a promotion. There is now more concern about the quality of living. "By cutting back on some of the regular household expenses, we feel we can still help our younger daughter in college."

Would you be willing to cut down on your household budget if it meant having a better quality of life? If it meant reducing the wrinkles on your face? How different are the pushing forces in your life today than they were last year at this time? Three years ago?

Analyzing the forces that keep you stuck or push you into change has given you a tool that can help manage the emotions and uncertainties of change. For some, making a lifestyle change is like eating an elephant—where do you begin? You begin by taking one bite at a time. Hopefully, by breaking your situation into individual forces, you will get fresh insights into what keeps you from reaching out and taking your life off hold.

You may find that some opposing forces are like an old, well-worn security blanket; you may not want to get rid of them. If you are a parent you probably remember your child dragging around an old dirty blanket that could never be replaced with a clean fresh one—it was like an old friend. Such is life—we hang on to some things because we are afraid to replace them with the new. So we remain stuck.

If there is one force in your life that you might compare to a security blanket, what would it be? How would you feel about giving up that old security blanket if it meant experiencing a more fulfilling life?

SECURITY

Security is illusive. We think we have it, but do we? It used to be thought that if you took a job with certain companies, such as Ma Bell, you had a job until you retired. Recent events have shown this is no longer true, as thousands of telephone workers find themselves being laid off. Mergers and acquisitions of companies have left top-management personnel looking for new jobs.

Today's reality is that you create your own security. Yet some people still cling to security as if it were the life force of their existence. Jim Stanley, an attorney, had this to say about security:

"Even after we had announced that we were going to leave Texas, we were still having some questions. Were we doing the right thing? We looked at the security of where we were. I looked at the security in my position. The way things were going, unless something very unexpected would have come up, I could have told you what I would be doing 20 years from now. We were ready to give up the security of the present for a new challenge."

For some, security represents a base from which to function. For others it represents being stuck. Since most people have a great need for security, businesses try to give their employees that secure feeling—until the day they are let go. That feeling of security means they are less likely to take out on their own. Businesses are filled with employees who would be a lot happier out on their own where they would have more freedom of movement, yet they stay right where they are because of security.

Bill and Heather Jarski, in their mid-30s, left Boston with their two young children and started a new life in a small scenic town where they have a store for custom-made furniture. Bill gave up the security of a very good job with Sears. What did his friends say about his leaving? "There were two different reactions. The older, more security-minded established group, the group that no matter how many times someone beat and kicked them, they are the ones who said, 'What are you doing giving up all those great benefits? You have profit sharing, medical, pension plan.' Then the other group on the other side of the fence was encouraging us to go for it."

What would you have said to Bill? Security is a powerful force that opposes change. It keeps our lives on hold. What are you giving up because of your need for security? What do you think would happen if you put less emphasis on security and more emphasis on doing what you want to accomplish in your life?

Have you ever stopped to think what gives you security?

Some people get their security in daily routine —getting up at the same time, driving to work on the same streets day after day, meeting the same people at the office, stopping off at the same grocery store where the clerks know them, eating the same time each day, sitting at the same place around the table, going to bed at the same time almost every night, after the same nightly ritual. It's comfortable. It doesn't take much thought. We can put our minds on automatic pilot.

Listen to people talk. They substitute words for security—routine, comfortable, predictable, familiar, always done it that way. What words or phrases would you add to the list? When making a lifestyle change—or a change of any sort—we give up that familiar routine.

My mother once told me how insecure she felt when she and Dad had to make a lifestyle change when they were in their early 40s. "Change is hard. It's terribly hard because you feel secure where you are. Just like when Daddy had to sell the cows because of our financial pressure. He had the cows on the sale bill and I walked outdoors and thought, all those cows are going to be sold and there goes our security. I wondered how I could help keep things going after the cows were gone—but we made it and now, 30 years later, I am so glad we did what we did, but it was very scary."

I felt the same way when I had to make a change after being fired. While there were some things about the job I didn't like and while I might have changed jobs later, at that moment I wasn't prepared to give up the security of a regular paycheck, insurance coverage and all the other perks. I was more emotionally prepared to hang in there than I was to make a change. Looking back, it was one of the best things that could have happened, but it didn't feel like it at the time.

Ellen Strain, a 26-year-old single mother, was forced into a major lifestyle change when her husband walked out on her. Ellen said, "I didn't realize my own potential. I was giving everything up to what I thought was security in my marriage."

In looking at the people around her, Ellen said, "They are afraid to change because they don't want to give up their security. It's hard to give up what you have. They think they will never find another man as good as this one, that it will be hard to find another job as good as this one, hard to find a place to live as good as this one. People want to be comfortable all the time. Changes are uncomfortable at first, but you grow from experiences. Want to have a crash course in getting over fear? Just have a divorce."

The more you believe in your own ability to make things happen, the less dependent you will be on security. The less you depend on security, the freer you will be to explore new options, which adds a new dimension to your life.

Do you feel free to explore options or is your perspective limited because you have been basking in security? This may explain why you feel stuck at times.

Change always stirs up feelings of risk and uncertainty. These uncertainties keep us stuck. We would rather tolerate an unpleasant situation than risk something new.

> "Freedom stretches only as far as the limits of our consciousness."
>
> —Carl Gustav Jung

RISK AND FEAR, TWO POWERFUL FORCES

Risk and fear are two major forces that can keep you stuck when considering making a lifestyle change. Imagine how much freer you would feel if you did not fear taking a risk. Risk does not have to be a threat

Fearing risk is like fearing a rose thorn. The rose attached to the stem is beautiful, but the thought of picking it is discouraged by the thought of getting pricked. Just as you can take a thorn apart piece by piece to make it lose its sting, you can take risk apart so that it loses its sting—and you lose your fear of it.

I saw a refreshing perception of risk at a senior citizen potluck supper where I met some of the live wires over 65. During the meal, some of them started talking about what it meant to live life to its fullest—which led to discussing risk.

One of the 75-year-old men was quite vocal in his feelings. "If you want to talk about risk, just look at the senior citizens who are crossing off the days on the calendar. Some people have been so cautious throughout their whole life that they mentally died before they reached retirement. The biggest risk people take is to do nothing." The man's wife chipped in by reminding us that the only difference between a rut and a grave is depth.

Ann McCann, housewife and mother of three sons, made a lifestyle change following a peaceful divorce after 35 years of marriage. Since her life changed she has become more aware of people who talk about what they want to do with their lives but don't do it. "It is important for people to do those things they always have wanted to do. If they find that what they thought they wanted to do doesn't measure up to expectations, then they can go on to the next thing. Each step opens the door to something else—it's part of the process of change."

Have you tried something, and even though it didn't work out as planned, it opened up a new door that wouldn't have been opened if you hadn't taken the initial steps? How do you look at risk as it applies to your life? Is it related to the fear of doing something new or of not doing anything? Are you overly cautious and stuck in a rut? Don't wait until that rut becomes a grave.

Risk Is Different For Everyone

This thing called *risk* is very complicated, as I discovered after an intensive 12-month study of the topic in graduate school. At the risk of sounding academic, here's what I found while researching my 225-page master's thesis.

"A Factor Analytic Study of Personality, Motivation and Risk-Taking Behavior" was a major study looking at risk from several perspectives. I had more than 200 students take a series of psychological tests plus some specially prepared risk-taking activities.

What were the findings after all this work? Nothing of any significant consequence. Why? Because risk appears to be multidimensional, with terrific emotional variation from one person to the next. The comparison could be made that a red car is always a red car, but a risk is not always a risk. For one person something may be a risk and for the next person it's not. Whether or not something is perceived as a risk involves our upbringing and our value and belief systems.

After my wife and I moved out here, one of my Texan friends remarked he wished he had the guts to make the kind of move we did. He said he really felt stuck where he was but didn't want to risk making a change. At ski areas, however, he thinks nothing of heading down expert slopes. While he describes my move as "gutsy," I wouldn't begin to risk skiing down an expert slope.

In fact, at my weekly ski lesson, the instructor once took the class down a steep slope with bumps. I couldn't handle it. I slid most of the way down on my rear rather than take the chance of hurting myself. Admittedly, it was somewhat humiliating, even more so as the other five students kept yelling back up at me to just let go and do it. I decided that when it comes to skiing, I wasn't going to try to be anyone's hero. I would rather be safe than sorry. Someday I will ski the expert slopes, but I will build up to it one step at a time. The important thing is to be taking those steps and not just sitting there thinking about it.

What are some of the things you consider risky that your friends seem to not think twice about doing—and vice versa? Why is it you feel these things are risky and they don't?

When Bill and Heather Jarski left Boston, some people thought they were risk takers, nonconformists. Heather responded, "We are not nonconformists. We did not participate in the student strikes in college during the Vietnam days. We were hiding in our dorms going, 'Oh my God it's crazy out there.' We obey all the laws, we don't speed, we are not inherent risk takers."

While Bill and Heather had led a rather traditional lifestyle up until this time, they were now ready to venture out. They weren't held back by what some would consider a risky decision. Risk is a strong force that has kept many people's lives on hold, as counsellor Allen Nesbitt pointed out, "I hear people talking about wanting to change but not doing it because of the risk—too many unknowns. People tell me how they hate what they are doing but then say 'I know it is secure and I don't have the guts to put myself and my family through the trauma.' People are unwilling to run the risk. Many have no sense of trust in their abilities."

How would you rate your level of trust in yourself when facing a risk? I didn't rate myself very high when I came down the ski slope the other day. As we reach out and try things and succeed at each minor step, we build personal trust in our abilities.

When you look at a risk situation, do you look at the probability of success or the probability of failure? One person will look at a new situation and say, there is a fifty-fifty chance of failure while another will refer to the situation as having a fifty-fifty chance of success. It gets back to looking at a glass as half full or half empty. Those who look at the glass as being half full are seeing things moving in a positive direction, while those seeing it empty are looking on the negative. While the difference may seem subtle, there is a big psychological difference.

When stockbrokers talk about a certain stock, they will say it has a 70 percent chance of going up significantly in the next year. Meanwhile, the person buying it is thinking about the 30 percent chance of it going down. That 30 percent possibility of it going down will cause some people not to buy, while the 70 percent chance of it going up will cause others to buy. The same information was given to both parties; they just evaluated it differently in terms of the risk involved.

Everyone approaches risk in different ways. Some learn to swim by jumping in the water the first day with the feeling that some way or the other, they won't drown. Others ease in and after several months they can swim. It is slower but safer for them.

Phil, 51, offered this advice to anyone considering making a change:

> "I would definitely say, 'Stay with your dream but don't just jump into something blindly.' When I quit my job and decided to buy a small store, I was so excited about it I didn't check it out very thoroughly, and I later discovered why the fellow was so friendly and interested in selling it. He had lied about the gross profits to expect, so instead of it being a moneymaker, it was a loser. Instead of it being a relaxing and enjoyable lifestyle change, it ended up being hell for the first three years."

Are you the kind of person who jumps in? Or do you take it more cautiously? Do you wish you were a bigger risk taker or less of one? If you changed your approach toward looking at risk, how might it affect the rest of your life?

As you look at the risk that is holding you back, ask yourself what you have to lose by taking that risk. What other information do you need before taking the risk? Who do you need to talk to, or what do you need to research to help get that information? Is it necessary for you to take the risk now? Or would it be better timing later? If yes, be sure you are not just procrastinating.

If you break a risk down into smaller parts, it will be more palatable. When making a lifestyle change, talk to others who have made a change like the one you are considering. How do they feel about their change? Are they glad they made it? Why? Would they do it over again? How do they think they might have lost out if they had not made their change?

I find in skiing that if I ski the mountain 12 inches at a time, I can handle it better than if I think of doing the whole slope at once. Likewise, take your risks a little at a time—it helps take away some of the fear.

Fear Paralyzes

While the uncertainty that comes with risk taking can stand as a roadblock to change, the fear that is generated in our minds can hinder our thinking or it can stimulate it to greater productivity. Usually, however, it hinders. Fear is a powerful force that directs your thoughts, controls your emotions and keeps your life on hold. It is natural to have some fear when considering making a change and facing the inherent uncertainties.

After a recent lifestyle change, 60-year-old psychotherapist Bob Hendrix found, "The fear of change is enough to cause people to paralyze themselves. There is the fear of the unknown and the fear of the known. Maybe they have taken a risk in the past and it didn't work out and now they are afraid to try it again. They may have the feeling that even though they are frustrated and would like to make the change, they don't want to take the risk. They prefer the security of the known."

Fear is much like a low-grade infection. It saps our energy. If you have a phobia, then you are aware of that specific fear and how it affects you. Other subtle fears also keep us stuck in a way of life that may be increasingly frustrating. What is amazing about fear is that the fear of something happening is normally worse than the actual event—to say nothing of the majority of the things we fear that never happen.

Take a look at the things you fear. Why do you have such fear of something bad happening? How are your fears keeping you from getting more out of life?

Harold, a 49-year-old executive, told how fear had crippled him in his business decisions. "When I had a big business deal coming up, I would spend way too much time worrying about what was going to happen. The time I spent worrying took away from the time I should have been preparing—so some of the things I feared came true."

When Harold began contemplating making a lifestyle change, he found his mind full of fears about the change. "I don't want to give up my life to a bunch of fears that may never happen," he said. "I am going to move ahead and trust that whatever happens, I will be able to handle it."

Imagine that the things you feared actually happened. Do you think you could handle them at that moment? Have you ever feared losing money and then lost it? While it was depressing and annoying and you wished you hadn't lost the money, you survived. Were you able to handle the situation better than you expected?

The more confidence you have in yourself, the less power fear will have as an opposing force. One of the best ways to overcome fear is to do what you are afraid of. The fears that I had when making a lifestyle change started disappearing with each step forward. Sitting around thinking about doing something is often more frightening than actually doing it.

THE PUSHING POWER OF CONFIDENCE

Confidence helps dissolve fears that keep our lives on hold. It adds strength to the pushing forces in our diagram. The greater our confidence, the less formidable are the opposing forces.

People making lifestyle changes have confidence in their abilities to handle the uncertainties of change. They don't let fear of the unknown stop them. Their comments reflect a belief that they can handle whatever might arise:

Diane Blessing, 37, who left one of the highest-paying school jobs in New Jersey, moved to the mountains and is now making sheepskin garments. "I don't worry because I know I can make it; I did in the past. It takes a strong personality to make a lifestyle change."

Jim Stanley, 48, an attorney who left Texas to seek new challenges in a new setting, is now assistant judge in a small town. "From the time I was 12, when I was buying my own clothes, I have had personal confidence to reach out and accept new challenges."

Jack Wells, a 40-year-old CPA, left a job at the Mayo Clinic to buy a bed-and-breakfast lodge. Jack saw different levels of confidence in his life. "I have always been extremely confident in my job, but not always so in other things. Let's face it, before making this change, work was a major portion of my life."

Marla Schneider, a 29-year-old mother of a four-year-old son moved from Toronto, Canada to "go into business with my older brother plus I didn't want my daughter to grow up in the city. I am a survivor. I feel wherever I am, I will be able to make ends meet and be able to meet financial and emotional crises."

How do you feel about your confidence in making a lifestyle change? Which is the stronger force in your life, fear or confidence?

Confidence might be compared to light and fear to darkness. As a boy, I hated to go outside at night to the outhouse because I was afraid the bears would get me—those proverbial bears that only come out at night. There was a marked contrast between my daylight confidence and my nighttime fears. Life would have been a lot easier if I had had as much confidence at night as I did during the day.

Just as you stumble around at night when there is no light, the same thing is true of your life. If you lack confidence, you stumble around. As your confidence increases, the fear of bears disappears. You are more ready to venture out.

If you lack confidence in your ability to find another job, you will be reluctant to leave your current job, even though you hate it. Three things might cause you to leave your job. You might build enough confidence in your ability to handle change that you finally decide to leave. Or you might become so dissatisfied with the job that you leave, regardless of your insecurities. Or you might be asked to leave. The first option, choosing to leave, gives you more control.

What are you putting up with right now that you would change if you had greater confidence? What are you doing to help build that needed confidence? When I lack confidence, I do a lot of reading and listening to motivational tapes. I find this helps me get out of an emotional rut.

Confidence is like a muscle. It needs to be exercised. Some people talk about confidence but never do anything to really check the muscle's ability. Others spend their time telling why they don't have confidence. It becomes a song and dance that justifies their lack of action. Which are you? Are you moving ahead or are you stuck?

Sometimes the thought of failure becomes so strong, it's like a sponge that absorbs our energy—energy that should be directed toward moving ahead. When this happens you need to look at how thoughts of failure affect your life.

"De-Catastrophize" the Thoughts of Failure

When you think of making a change, does the thought of failure stand as a roadblock to your moving ahead? How would your life be different if you could dissolve that fear and reach out for a new quality of living?

Some people stay stuck in a frustrating, depressing situation because they are afraid of failure. The fear of failure hangs over them like a dark cloud that keeps the sun out.

While you may fail at something, that does not make you a failure. This is an important distinction. While your project may receive an *F*, it does not mean you receive an *F* as a human being.

Children, with their free spirits, can teach us a lot about getting out of ruts in our lives. They are not paralyzed by a fear of risk. Just think how our lives would have been different if we had been afraid to take an early risk. It's unlikely we would have learned to walk.

Have you ever watched a young child taking his or her first steps? What a lesson in risk taking. I was intrigued when my 12-month-old grand-nephew, Josh, tried to take his first steps. He slowly pulled himself up the arm of the sofa, then leaned out from the sofa and started to take a step—then fell on his soft rear. After looking around at the excited expressions on his parents' faces, he slowly crawled back to the arm of the sofa and tried again and again and again, until he finally took a couple steps. There was no fear of failure. His self-worth was not bruised with each fall; rather, he went right back and tried it again and again. What a lesson for adults.

Some people have an overwhelming fear of failure. Such is the case with Fred Deppner, 43, whose successful business took a drastic drop, going from 33 employees to one. "I am scared to death of failure and suppose that some people would say what I have accomplished would be success in their book. We have all been in situations where we have a special challenge and we don't make the challenge—it's a devastating feeling. The pit of your stomach drops and all those butterflies and bad things feel horrible. I just hate those feelings, so I would always do whatever I had to do. I didn't want to fail."

What is Fred's advice to those with a similar fear of failure? "If you find yourself in a tight situation, exercise is very important to help relieve tension. Then back up and look at the situation and write down a worst-case scenario. What is the worst thing that might happen? Often the worst-case scenario really isn't that bad when you look at it—it really isn't a life-or-death situation—you are still alive."

But what happens if things don't work out? It's not the end of the world even though it may seem like it is. One way to help reduce the paralyzing effects of fear is to remind yourself that even a worst-case scenario is not a catastrophe. "De-catastrophizing" the worst takes away some of fear's venom. You move past the feeling that it's the end of the world. You are able to move on with your life.

Marvin Heppner, 49, has had several business disappointments that might have made another person want to jump off a bridge. But Marvin hung in there.

"A lesson I have learned from my ups and downs is how trapped we get by fear. It is a big waste of energy. I think with people who are afraid to make a change because of fear, their fear is unjustified. When I think of the fear I had in my early career and the changes I made, that fear would not have had to be there. Later on I didn't have as much fear. I just jumped in and did it. I am excited about the changes in the future and I have no fear at all. I look at people who have that fear and see there is no reason for it. I have some friends who were afraid to make a change. Then after they did it, they were surprised how smooth it went, and before, they had spent time stewing about it."

Do you find that you spend time fearing situations—"stewing" about them—then later realize it wasn't nearly as bad as you had feared? Have you ever almost not done something because of fear, then gone ahead and done it and were glad you did? How is your life different today because of it?

Clarence, 41, made a lifestyle change at age 34 when he left his position as manager of a large retail store and went for a college degree. "I had wanted to get a college degree for years, but I was afraid I wasn't smart enough so I kept putting it off. I finally decided to jump in and give it my best shot. I'm glad I did. I wonder how much further I would have gone by now if my life hadn't always been controlled by fear."

Some people live with the fear that something terrible is going to happen and their whole life will be ruined. Such a fear keeps their lives in a rut. They are afraid to venture out. To help overcome the paralysis of fear, we can learn from those who have been faced with it and how they moved through the barrier.

Such a person is Ken Unruh, a Denver psychotherapist. He was afraid that while everything was going great now, he might lose it. And that's what happened. Although it was a painful experience that almost ended his life, he now describes it as a freeing experience. Ken believes the rest of his life will have greater quality and richness because of what he learned about himself and life as a result of this experience.

"Three years ago I had everything. I was successful in my career, I was happily married, I was enjoying leisure time, I was developing properties. A year later, everything started tumbling—my marriage, my financial security, my investments. I ended up declaring bankruptcy with $35 in my pocket, a 12-inch TV, a waterbed, sofa and two chairs. My assets had crumbled from an estimated $850,000 net worth to nothing.

"When things started to crumble, I felt I was losing control no matter how innovative I was or how hard I worked. My survival had never been tested before. When marriage and business all came under attack, I couldn't control the losses. I began to wonder about my basic judgment, whether I was insane, crazy.

"I feared losing my physical health. I started having all kinds of symptoms. My heart was fluttering and I feared I was going to have a heart attack and what if I am dying and there is no one around to hear my cry. I was experiencing sleeplessness, which is very unusual for me. I was losing weight and went from having to watch my weight to having to eat four meals a day to keep my weight up.

"It was a great battle being waged in my mind. It was an enormous struggle over my basic self-esteem. I was facing the evil effects of fear, doubt, death, upset with myself, blaming myself, the whole range of negative, destructive thoughts.

"I remember driving about 90 miles an hour and seeing a bridge abutment ahead of me. It looked extremely attractive to head right into it. It was a frightening moment because I was entertaining the idea at a level I had never entertained before. I felt trapped; I felt I had no options; I didn't know a way out.

"I can't tell you how hard I worked, in my reflection and self-examination, to determine a perspective about life and existence. Friends were a help. I went to see a therapist, which was very necessary, and I spent a lot of time reading and re-reading the Book of Job from the Bible. Job had love, a family, children, wife and enormous material holdings. Suddenly, like me, everything crumbled for him. He kept asking God, "What have I done?" I had the same question.

"When one has experienced major losses and changes, it is important to select some daily activity that can have meaning and fulfillment that will help rebuild one's self-worth. I committed myself for training for a marathon—at age 46. All I needed was a pair of trunks and jogging shoes. I put an effort into that each day and it was an arena where I could experience considerable fulfillment, mastery and achievement.

"From having lost everything, I am starting to rebuild. I now know that I have a wholeness, a completeness as a human being. I am a stronger personality. I have more tools to come back to myself when I can't find sustenance from the outside, whether it is material or personal. From my struggle, I have gained a new belief in my ability to handle adversity. I am now aware of many more options to reaching fulfillment in life.

"When you get down to basic self-existence, it is important to have a goal that you can focus on for that day, for that week, for that month. These goals need to be realistic and attainable. When you master goals, no matter how small, it becomes self-perpetuating, self-fulfilling. You develop self-confidence, positive thought. You then are ready to take on another goal. You can always come back to something you can control. With these successes, the more fully and completely you will trust yourself, and you will feel more whole. With your feeling of goodness, it will be easier to move on to experience a new quality of life.

"Most people have a fear of failing. While no one wants to intentionally fail, the fear involved is less manageable than the actual occurrence. We give much of our lives up to fear. People have greater strength to come through adversity than they realize."

After listening to Ken's story, I was reminded of Romans 5: 3,4— from the Bible,

". . .We rejoice in our sufferings knowing that suffering produces endurance, and endurance produces character, and character produces hope."

People who have gone through personal trauma confirm that the fear of something happening was greater than the actual event. Why? Fear's domain is the future, where we have little control. Have you ever gotten ready to go on an extended trip by car? Does the fear of the car breaking down ever cross your mind? Some people refuse to even start on a trip because of that fear. If that doesn't happen to be your fear, you may not understand why these people are so afraid of car problems. Likewise, those who have made lifestyle changes may not understand why others have such fear of change.

If you are a person who worries about your car breaking down you usually imagine it out in the middle of nowhere. There you are—helpless. Although I recognize the frailty of cars and am concerned about breakdowns, I'm not so concerned that it keeps me from traveling. This year the transmission on our two-year-old foreign-make car broke down out in the middle of nowhere. The fear that had crossed my mind happened. In my fear, however, I didn't visualize that there would be a farmer a mile away that was making hay, and that he would graciously take me to his home where I could call a wrecker. There also happened to be a mechanic in the town 20 miles away who could work on our car. It took five weeks to get the car fixed, and we went by bus and plane instead of car—but we adapted. The episode was an annoyance but not something so bad that it deserved any "fear time."

At Christmas time, our other car, another foreign-make, broke down. The tow truck operator wanted $750 just to take it to the nearest qualified mechanic. When fearing such an expensive breakdown, which was about to become reality, my thinking hadn't pictured a nephew who was coming through the next day on his way to Breckenridge and could take us back. I hadn't pictured a farmer and his wife who agreed to load the car on the back of one of their farm trailers and take it to a mechanic in trade for staying in our condo. Again, the breakdown was an annoyance, but it wasn't so bad that it deserved any upfront "fear time."

What fears do you have that are keeping your life on hold? Take those fears and add some good news to them. If you fear a car breakdown, see it happening in front of the house of the best and least-expensive mechanic in the state. See the new friends you made as your car is being worked on. If you want to make a lifestyle change that requires a geographic move, visualize the excitement of meeting stimulating people who will open other new doors in your life.

Have you found things often work out better than you expect? Have you found that, regardless of how bad a situation may be, one way or another you are able to work through it and in many cases come out much better than you anticipated in your fears?

People have an amazing ability to rise to the occasion. Yet in the fearful thoughts that keep them awake at night, they don't give themselves the credit they deserve. You need to realize that you have the ability and potential to meet the challenge of the moment without worrying about what might happen. Fear is a crippler. It is an emotion that can keep you from being able to move ahead with your life.

When making a lifestyle change you can analyze and evaluate the uncertainty of the future and then take the steps to move ahead. Or you can sit there and be afraid to walk through the door, and then look back on your life when you are 75 and ask yourself, "Why didn't I go through the door?" You might have the same regrets as Hank, 67, a former banker:

"On my 65th birthday, I retired. While it should have been an exciting time, it was depressing to me because it seemed I let my life slip by me because I was afraid to try anything. I worked for the same bank for 41 years, which was impressive to some. They gave me a nice gold watch with a couple diamonds on it, but I would rather have had other experiences and they could have kept their watch. But it is my own fault I didn't. My wife encouraged me to explore some other work when I was 50, but I felt I was too old to risk it. Now I wish I would have at least checked some things out. My lack of confidence and fear kept me right where I was."

It is not death that a man should fear, but he should fear never beginning to live.

—Marcus Aurelius

Do you feel stuck by fear? Here is a little exercise that has helped some people break away from fear. In the previous chapter, in-depth instructions were given on how to help you visualize something you want in your life. Use that same approach to visualize yourself in a fearful situation. While you are in that situation, see yourself being able to handle it. See options arising that turn it into a good situation. If you fear being turned down for a job, visualize yourself going in to apply, seeing the interviewer liking what you have to offer and giving you the job. Don't spend time thinking you won't be hired. Negative visualization just adds more fear to your life.

Realize that whatever happens will never be so bad you can't handle it. Trust yourself. Tell yourself over and over, "I am not going to fear what is going to happen in the future. I know that whatever it is I can handle it because I have handled it in the past."

Your being able to handle it may include going to see a counselor or reading a book that speaks to your concerns. Give yourself permission to consider that if you really got down and out, you would not be embarrassed to go see a counselor. As you read this book, you will meet several individuals who felt stuck in their emotions and were helped by going to see a counselor who helped them get a clearer picture of the situation. I have heard people say, "You would never catch me going to a counselor." Meanwhile they stay stuck in their muddle. Sometimes having the assurance that you can handle anything also means you are not too proud to get assistance. Asking for help is better than sitting in your fear and doing nothing.

Even though Ken Unruh was a psychotherapist, he turned to outside help when he was faced with the terrific tension of his losses. He knew it was hard to clearly see his own situation. If your worst fears came to pass, you too would find a way to get through it. And more likely than not, your fears will never be realized in the first place.

People who go through trying situations recap the experience in terms of seeing more options now, having a greater faith in their own abilities, having a greater appreciation of life and being more relaxed. These are quite different terms than those used to describe something that is feared—words like catastrophe, terrible, not sure I could handle it, failure, devastating, helpless —words that have a lot of emotional energy attached to them. What words do you tend to use most? What does that tell about you?

> I believe that anyone can conquer fear by doing the things he fears to do, provided he keeps doing them until he gets a record of successful experiences behind him.
> —Eleanor Roosevelt

THEY WANTED TO CHANGE BUT DIDN'T

Harold and his wife, June, have a prosperous business. During the past year they have thought about making a major lifestyle change—which would include a geographic move. For a couple of reasons, including their children, they think it's best to wait. A former teacher, June has had students she felt were very unsettled because they had been moved around. She doesn't want that to happen to their children.

This still gives Harold and June the option of making a lifestyle change without moving. Yet at this point they prefer to keep the business—even with all its pressures. Why? An interweaving of value systems keeps them plugging away, even though they admit they might be financially ahead if they sold.

Harold and June did a careful evaluation of the forces that were pushing for and opposing their making a change. Harold's forces, along with the values he gave each one, were as follows:

PUSHING FORCES		OPPOSING FORCES
tired of hustle and bustle of city	9 >	< 8 fear of unknown concerning financial ramifications
stuck in a rut in career	6 >	< 7 drastic change may affect children
current lifestyle requires income	5 >	< 8 would miss friends too much
not enough time for doing what I like	7 >	
		< 1 families would add pressure
		< 1 pressure to keep company successful
		< 10 haven't reached aspiration point of company
27 Total		35 Total

In June's evaluation, some of the pushing forces relate to her desire to leave hot Texas weather and move to a small mountain town.

PUSHING FORCES		OPPOSING FORCES
want to see Harold	10 >	< 9 child in college happy
want less tension	8 >	< 8 two more to send to college
want prettier scenery	6 >	< 6 not sure what I want
want less hot weather	5 >	< 5 am afraid of change
want less congestion	6 >	< 9 will miss friends
want less to take care of around the house	7 >	< 8 feel needed in business
want more free time	8 >	< 7 hate to leave church and home
want quality family time	9 >	
59 Total		52 Total

While Harold's opposing forces are stronger than his pushing forces, June's pushing forces are stronger than her opposing forces. Because neither June nor Harold wants to make a change right now, there are probably additional opposing forces that June didn't think of or the values she assigned to the different forces don't completely reflect her core feelings.

One of June and Harold's big concerns relates to their business. When asked why they didn't sell, Harold responded, "I think whenever you go into business you start out with an aspiration. It may be very simple and straightforward. Somewhere after a year or so your aspirations change, and you have a new aspiration point which is probably more realistic than the one you started with. That aspiration point is real important. I think at some point, whenever you start thinking about selling the business or getting out of the business, you have got to be sure you gave it everything you could to reach that aspiration point. If you haven't reached it, then you are probably going to be hesitant to get out. That aspiration point has a financial value and it also has career value."

June, who takes an active part in the business, added, "I feel we have a goal and I don't feel we have reached it with the company. I have never been a quitter. When I came into the company two and a half years ago as manager, my objective was to get everything straightened out so Harold could spend more time selling—I don't have everything straightened out yet.

"Between the two of us, we should be able to do it. It is hard to give it up until we get to a certain point. We offer the best service and it would be hard to find someone who would carry it on like we have. However, I also don't think it is worth it to kill the two of us trying to do it."

When asked, "If you had six months to live, would you make a change?"

June replied quickly, "Yes, if I had months to live I don't think I would live it the way I am doing."

Harold chuckled. "I would be out on the golf course every day."

My next question was, "Are you giving up your life for a god called 'aspiration'?"

Harold answered, "Everybody has to have aspirations."

June added, "I am not sure why I think it is worth it right now. This is something that has been going over and over in my mind for the last year. I don't really know that it is worth it. All I know is that we have to choose the time to do whatever we are going to do. I think we have both decided that our business is not worth it and it is not what we want to do, but we have to choose the right time to get out."

Harold closed the interview with an analogy he thought summarized their thinking and values. "It's kind of like a baseball team. You go into the season and you want to come into first place. Somewhere along the way you are going to lose a few games and you are going to win a few games. But the season is not over. We don't want to give up until the season is over. What I am saying is that there are still some games to be won and some games to be lost out there and we are going to hang in there. Now we may not sign up and play next season, but we don't want to give up in the middle of the season, so to speak. It's a matter of timing."

Harold and June are motivated to hang in there. At the same time they recognize they would not want to spend the last six months of their lives stuck in their business. Good business sense is a value that emphasizes the importance of timing—it's good business sense that may be in conflict with quality of life.

SUMMARY: THOUGHTS ON THE FORCES OF CHANGE

When I asked people why they thought their friends would not be willing to make lifestyle changes like they did, their replies included:

"People are worried about security."

"People have roots and it's hard to leave."

"It takes a strong personality to make such a change."

"They are stuck in a rut."

"They're afraid of not being able to make new friends."

The most common response was, "They would be afraid of the risk."

Those who have made changes do not feel it was that big of a risk. Risk is different for different people. Have you ever done things that your friends would never risk doing, and vice versa?

Risk suggests uncertainty. To reduce the perceived risk, get as much information as possible. If you are afraid to change your lifestyle because you don't know how the change might affect you, then talk to someone who has already made the change. The goal of this book is to give you input from others who have made a lifestyle change and are willing to share their gut-level feelings about the change. They did it, so can you—if the desire is there.

When those who have let go and made changes reflect back on their fears, they see how they wasted their time worrying. How much time did you spend worrying today instead of enjoying your family or your surroundings? Did you find that you failed to pay attention to the task of the moment because you were worrying about something in the future?

You will move through your fears more easily when you break them into component parts that are more manageable and workable. This process helps make the fears more objective and less subjective. You then can deal with the component parts one step at a time rather than "eating the whole elephant at once. "

When dealing with risk, our train of thought often goes from focusing on the risk, to focusing on the fear of the risk, to focusing on the fear of failing when risks are taken. We end up focusing on fear of failure, which creates an impasse in our thinking. As attested to by those interviewed, failing is no fun, but it is not worth giving up your life worrying about it.

People who have faced failure have found they are resilient enough to handle more than they thought. They began to see other options. They turned to sources of help to make it through the difficult times—books, counselors, prayer, friends. The important thing is that they made it. Not only did they make it, they now are stronger and more resourceful. They have a stronger appreciation of life and of their own internal strength. Their experiences support Napoleon Hill's philosophy, "Every adversity, every failure and heartache carries with it the seed of an equivalent or a greater benefit."

A decision-making tool that helps when making a change is to separate out the different pushing and retarding forces that surround your change. This gives you smaller pieces to work with. By objectifying each force and giving it a value, you take away some of the subjective uncertainty and fear. It goes back to the concept of how to eat an elephant—one bite at a time.

The thought of change can make you especially tense if another person in your life says, "Don't even think about change." To get through the impasse, have the other person do a force analysis describing how they see the situation. See how the forces affecting it for them compare with yours. Then discuss how each feels about each of the forces you described. Here is where good listening and patience come in to play.

The good news is that there are tools to help you walk through your lifestyle change—or any other type of change you may be contemplating. You have more ability to handle the perceived risk than you imagined. Just don't let your fear cripple you from even wanting to try. Men, here is a time to forget that your dad said to be a big boy or to not be afraid. If you have fears, share them. It's much better to share your fears, because doing so opens the door for communication and clarifies your thinking.

It is important for all of us to experience our feelings rather than denying that they exist. Too often, unpleasant feelings are denied through the use of alcohol or drugs. When we deny our feelings, we stay stuck and never walk through the door to our next experience. While it may seem trite to say it, the reality is that we have only one life to live and it is now.

ACTIVITIES AND QUESTIONS TO HELP OVERCOME THE FEAR OF CHANGE

The following activities and questions are designed to help you overcome the fear of change.

1. To evaluate the pushing forces and the opposing forces related to the change you are considering, use the following diagram to help you clarify your thinking. On the left side, write down the reasons you would like to change. You do not

have to use all the lines—or you may need to draw more. Likewise, on the right-hand side, list the reasons that are holding you back from changing.

PUSHING FORCES   OPPOSING FORCES

_____ > < _____

_____ > < _____

_____ > < _____

_____ > < _____

_____ > < _____

_____ > < _____

_____ > < _____

Total _____   Total_____

Now look at both sides of the diagram and decide which force is the strongest. Give it a value of 10. Although you do not need a 10 on each side, it may end up that you have them. You do need at least one 10 to set your upper extremes. Now, pick out the least powerful force and give it a value of one. Again, this is looking at the total diagram, not individual sides. With those two forces as the extremes, give each of the remaining forces a value between one and 10.

Total up the value of each side. Do the totals agree with what you are doing in your life? If the pushing side has the larger total, yet you are not making a change, then you have overlooked some important force or you have not correctly valued the impacts of different forces in your life. The other possibility is that you are just procrastinating? If so, why?

2. What are some risks that make you uptight? What are some risks that would make someone else uptight but don't seem to bother you? What does this tell you about yourself?

3. What are some things you once feared and now don't even think twice about? What made the difference? How can that reduction in fear be transferred to what you now fear?

4. Think of something that you once feared you could not handle, yet when it happened you made it. What did you learn about fear from that experience?

5. If you were giving a lecture to a group of people who were your age, what five points would you make about overcoming fear? Are you using those points yourself or do they just sound good? Why aren't you using them?

6. What things have happened in your life that at one time you would have called failures? Why did you call them failures back then? How has your thinking changed about failure? What lessons have you learned from these so-called failures?

7. Of the different personal accounts you read in this chapter, which one made the biggest impression on you? Why do you think that is?

8. If someone asked you how you look at risk and fear differently since reading this chapter, what would you tell them?

9. Think of one thing you are afraid of doing and then decide to do it. Let this be the beginning of overcoming fear. As you go through the fear situation, pay close attention to how you feel. Are your palms sweating? What did you learn about yourself? Why didn't you try it before?

10. How do you feel when you share your feelings with others? Why don't you do it more often? Can you think of a time that you had some pent-up feelings and when you expressed them, you felt much better? Would you agree that when you really get in touch with your bad feelings, it helps you move ahead in your daily living because it keeps you from being stuck with hashing and rehashing?

TAKE YOUR LIFE OFF HOLD

Having read this far, you now have the major ingredients for making a lifestyle change. Next comes the emotional energy that you use to stir these ingredients. Emotional energy acts as yeast to make the ingredients rise and take shape.

Hopefully by now your juices are flowing. You have learned how you can begin to create the lifestyle you are searching for. Hopefully you feel a new release of energy inside you. Perhaps your friends are saying you are too enthusiastic and they wish you would calm down a little. Don't worry about it. Based on my experience with supervising people, I would rather cool down a fanatic than warm up a corpse.

Admittedly, some people have more energy than others. From the day they were born they had more energy. They were the hyperactive children who became the high-energy adults. Other people have energy on some days and not on others, depending on how things are going for them. Some days are just more emotionally draining than others.

The energy you bring to a lifestyle change depends on the harmony and peace of mind you feel. It depends on your understanding of yourself and what gives you energy and what takes it away. It depends on your feelings of self-worth and personal confidence. It depends on the attitude you bring to life in general. This is exciting because it depends upon you, not someone else. Many of the other ingredients needed to make a lifestyle change interact with outside factors. But when it comes to attitude and the energy you bring to life, you're the one in control.

74

Right now you may feel overwhelmed, not knowing where to begin. You may feel that the ideas you have played around with in your mind are beyond you. They are just too big of a challenge. You may feel like a person trying to eat an elephant. Where do you begin? You begin by taking one bite at a time.

IS YOUR CHALLENGE AN ELEPHANT OR A CHICKEN?

When our challenges get too big, they can get out of control unless we know how to handle them—and they can be handled.

Last Christmas I helped put the Christmas tree up at church. It was a beautiful, 25-foot tree that had been cut from the mountainside. We got the tree inside, and I was to push it up as the other man held the base. Weaving my hand through the prickly pine needles, I found the trunk. I slowly started pushing the tree upright, but when it got halfway up, it started wobbling all over, and ended up coming down on top of me. The next attempt was more systematic—and it worked. It was a good feeling to have conquered the big tree, instead of vice versa.

The same is true with lifestyle changes. You may feel out of control and wonder if it is all worth it. You may think it is easier to just keep your life on hold and let come what comes. Think again—you can do it. Perhaps you have forgotten how big some challenges looked to you as a kid.

Do you remember when your mother told you to clean your room? Where did you begin? To me it looked like an avalanche. It was easy to want to give up and just lie in bed and look at the mess. Mother worked out a plan: Pick everything up off the floor and put it on the bed—which made it impossible for me to lie down—then take one item off the bed at a time and put it away. The system worked—and it always felt good to have a clean room.

When considering a lifestyle change you may want to just lie there and think about the change. You're overwhelmed. If so, you need to mentally put things on the bed so you can't lie back down. Then you need to mentally take them off until everything is in its place. That is a major key to handling big challenges—break them down so they are manageable. Work out a system that helps you reach the goal you want.

Some people cheat themselves by going for a smaller goal than what they really want. Rather than trying to eat an elephant, they go for a chicken. Rather than trying to figure out how to put up a 25-foot Christmas tree, they go for a six-foot tree—or they cut the 25-foot tree into smaller pieces, which destroys the purpose of getting a big tree in the first place.

For people used to working with big goals, going for just a chicken means they miss the challenge. Such was the case with Gerald and Margaret Devine, who, in their mid-50s, sold their truck stops for an opportunity to spend more time in the mountains. After a while, they missed the excitement of the competitive business world. Gerald said, "We don't regret our lifestyle change for a minute. However, I'm not sure how long I want to continue this lifestyle. I really miss the excitement and challenge of business. I would kind of like borrowing a half-million dollars and starting over again." Since the time of this interview, Margaret has taken on a jewelry line that she sells to stores and Gerald has gone to work for an insurance company. Too much of a good thing can get boring.

As you look at your life goals, are they "chicken-sized" or "elephant-sized"? Are you short-changing yourself? Energy for living comes from challenges—not from coasting. It comes from having a purpose for your life and from your accomplishments.

WALKING ON THORNS

Imagine that you are walking barefooted through a patch of sharp thorns. With each step you take, the pain becomes more excruciating. This happened to me once, and I didn't know whether to go forward or back. What I wanted to do was sit down and scream, but there was no place to sit down.

Now imagine that you are on the other side of those thorns. You look across the thorns and see a child about to be hit by a car. You go dashing across the thorns and grab the child just in time. Did you feel the thorns? Probably not at the time you went dashing across them. All your attention was focused on saving the child.

Likewise, if you have your attention focused on some purpose in your life, you won't feel the thorns you have to walk across to get there. If you don't have a purpose, you will be concentrating on your sore feet. A purpose in life takes away the fear of getting there.

Many people's lives are kept on hold because all the people can see are the thorns. Without purpose you don't feel as well. You have more aches and pains. All your attention is focused on you rather than on where you are going.

Have you ever come home from work feeling like you couldn't take another step? Then someone calls and asks if you would like to play a game of tennis, and, all of a sudden, you feel a new release of energy. Where did that come from? It came from your anticipation of winning that game. You had purpose. You were ready for the challenge.

When Jim Cavin was 40, he left his position in sales and marketing with Reynolds Aluminum to come to Breckenridge. This was back in the early 1970s when there wasn't much here. He related the importance of understanding the direction and purpose of his life: "When you reach the age of 40, which was my age when I made my big change, you make some pretty important decisions about yourself—what you want to be, where you want to go, where you want to do it." Jim now owns part of a multi-million-dollar real estate development firm.

Is your life on hold because you haven't taken time to look at what your purpose is and what direction you want to take? If you could put it in one sentence, what would you say is the purpose of your life? What relationship do you see between your statement of purpose and your self-worth?

SELF-WORTH, THE FUEL FOR CHANGE

People making lifestyle changes have a strong sense of self-worth that gives them the confidence to reach out for what they want. Their self-confidence made them willing to get outside the stale security of their comfort zone.

Chris Litsey, 35, had been the vice president of a successful retail firm. He gave up his high-stepping lifestyle to give massages at an exclusive resort club. He's also a guide on whitewater rafting trips. In his work he meets a lot of doctors, lawyers and other professionals—people who are intrigued by his new lifestyle. They tell him how they would like to change their lifestyles and get rid of their tensions and frustrations but they don't. Why? "They admit they are afraid to give up their security," says Chris. "They don't want to get outside their comfort zone."

From his lifestyle change, Chris has discovered, "You have to rely on yourself 100 percent. Many people have not relied on themselves, so they don't know whether they have what it takes or not. They are used to business situations where they rely a lot on other people."

It takes a strong sense of self-worth to have the confidence to rely on yourself. What situations have you had in your life that required you to rely heavily on yourself? How did you do? Did you discover some things about yourself in the process?

In his best-selling book, *The Road Less Traveled*, Scott Peck wrote, "Problems call forth our courage and our wisdom; indeed, they create our courage and wisdom. It is only because of problems that we grow mentally and spiritually."

Chris took a fresh look at his self-worth during his change. "For me to resign my position, to sell my motor home and everything I equated with status, was to peel away all the superfluous layers of who I thought I was and find out who I really was. I was forced to meet myself—what I am made of, what I am capable of. It was to take a fresh look at my self-worth."

As Chris recognized, a lifestyle change helps us take a new look at ourselves. It can be refreshing—or it can be humbling. Which would be your case? At times, things happen that momentarily destroy our self-worth, leaving us not knowing what to do next. When our self-worth is threatened, the very core of our existence is threatened. It can take away our lifeblood if we let it.

Self-Worth Wrapped up in Titles

How would your self-worth be affected if your title were stripped from you? How much of your self-worth is wrapped up in your title? Some people cling to their titles as if that were their only worth.

It's often hard to give up a title, as Chris Litsey discovered. "Even a year or two after leaving my vice-president's job, I carried some of my old cards and when someone would ask for a card, to impress them I would give them one with my vice-president title on it. I was still clinging to who I was, not who I am."

Let's imagine you were just made vice-president of a bank. Are you a better person now that you are a vice-president than you were before getting the title? You may have some new fringe benefits, but are you a better person? Conversely, are you a lesser person if you lose your title?

While in Africa I saw firsthand the danger of getting hung up on titles. It happened on the way to a training conference. Several of us rode to the conference with an officer of the United States Information Agency. On the way, we were stopped by a group of militant locals. We were ordered out of the Land Rover, which infuriated the service officer. He started shouting that they couldn't stop us because he was an officer with the American Information Service. They could not have cared less. Another fellow and I calmed the officer down before we had a major incident. Clearly, the only thing that was going to help us get out of that mess was how we reacted to their request—not some title they didn't understand.

Is your self-worth all wrapped up in your title? Is your life on hold because of your title? Some companies have found that a good way to keep employees is to give them new titles every so often—many times without raises. It's a way to play on their vanity.

A number of people interviewed for this book mentioned friends who probably would never make a lifestyle change because they were so proud of the title they had in their job—even though the pay wasn't that great. Gary mentioned a 45-year-old friend who was the executive vice president of an Ohio bank. "My friend was saying he would like to make a change and when I asked why he didn't, he said he always dreamed about being an executive vice-president and hated to give it up at this point in his life."

It didn't bother Rick Hum, 41, when he gave up his title as vice-president at CitiBank in New York. He had been the youngest person in the history of the bank to get that title, and only the second person in the history of the bank to get the title when under the age of 30. The first was John Reed, now chairman of Citicorp. Rick gave up the title to take on a slower-paced life. "If I had stayed there I would probably have been sick and crazy. I was already getting an ulcer. There is more to life than ulcers." Rick is now a computer consultant who also teaches at the local college.

While teaching at a university, Amy Jordan, Ph.d., discovered how important titles are to some educators. "They are notorious for holding on to a title acquired in years past, such as assistant dean. They will stay in that position as long as they can hold on to it."

Lillian, 75, observed, "I am always surprised when a doctor introduces himself as Doctor so-and-so. It always makes me think they think they are more important than their patient. If it wasn't for us, they would go hungry." While subtle, how we introduce ourselves tells how much of our self-worth is tied up with our titles. While you can't eat titles, they do feed our egos.

Is your self-worth strong enough that you would be willing to give up your title to do something that paid less and you enjoyed more?

John found he couldn't. For a while he thought about giving up his high-pressure position as vice-president of manufacturing and doing what he really liked doing best—gardening. "When I mentioned to some of my friends about giving up my vice-president's job and doing yard work, you should have seen their looks. This made me wonder, would I be doing the right thing? It definitely would be different to introduce myself as a gardener instead of as the vice-president of manufacturing."

After much thought, John decided to stay where he is. He is not ready to make the change. Money is not the reason, for he has enough to get by. Rather, it's that he has worked a long time to get the title and hates to give it up just yet. What would you have done in this situation?

Frank Moran, 50, reflected back on his 13 years of banking experience, remembering how important titles were to him back then. "People who work in banks think that titles are the greatest thing in the world. They don't make much money but they love those titles. They would rather hang on to a title than try something new. One of the biggest problems people have is their own ego."

It is important to add, however, that many people are in occupations because they love their work, not because of a title, status or the size of the desk. Just remember, seldom do they put titles on tombstones.

I remember how I felt when I sold my company and no longer had a title. I went through an identity crisis. How do you establish your identity when someone asks what you do? Do you tell them you are exploring life? Do you say you are semi-retired at age 48? Or do you make up some socially acceptable story—that you are exploring other business opportunities? Back then, what I really wanted to say was that it is really not important what I do; it is more important who I am.

How much of your emotional energy is tied up in your title? How does your title affect your decision to make a lifestyle change? Could you handle just having your name without the added prestige of a title?

Your Worth—Your Job

How much of your self-worth is wrapped up in the fact that you have a certain job or profession? What would it do to your self-worth if you had a lesser job? Jobs often are our armor. For many, if they couldn't talk about their work, they wouldn't have anything to say. Their work is the source of their identity. To maintain that image they work harder and harder. Does that sound familiar?

According to psychotherapist Bob Hendrix, "Directly or indirectly, all of us are taught we are what we produce and if we don't produce anything we are not worth anything. You see people who have that concept who continue to produce and they don't take time to develop the other areas of their lives."

How are you developing the other areas of your life? Is your self-worth all wrapped up in your job? What words would you use to describe your self-worth if you couldn't talk about what you do? Is your self-worth based on your title, your checkbook, what your friends think of you, what you do?

"When I resigned from my vice president's position, a lot of my friends disappeared," said Chris Litsey. "I no longer had the status symbols as in position, Mercedes, motor home. My friends wanted to be around people who had the success image. My values have changed since those days."

Society puts a lot of weight on what we do—are we in a position of prestige and power or are we in a basic job? Henry, 61, remembered how important his job had been to him. He was trapped in the power, the image of being the president of a medium-sized advertising firm.

"I don't think I would have admitted this 10 years ago, before my heart problems, but I needed the status of my job to keep me going. I was the youngest of six boys and, as you can see, I am short—only 5 feet, 9 inches. I always felt like the underdog. When I got to be president, I had a new image with my family and others.

"Because of all the pressure at the agency, my wife encouraged me to step down, but I liked being looked up to, being called president. After my heart attack, I realized how much of my life was wrapped up in what I was doing. That started a change in my thinking. Since having resigned my position, I am aware of people who were friends because of what I did rather than who I was. That was a real eye-opener."

Others who have made job changes have found the same thing to be true. When all our worth is tied up in what we do, it is hard to give that up.

Sometimes it's hanging on to roles that keeps our lives on hold. Carolyn Lohman, who at age 43 went back to college to get a degree in counseling, sees some women lacking their own identity because they hang on to their roles. "I know women who only have connection with their role as Mrs. so-and-so or being the wife of such and such executive or the mother of this or that kid. They have lost connection with the real person inside—that vital being who is sensitive to her own humanity. They shop, they play tennis, they stay busy. At the same time, they feel a vacuum of not having a special identity of their own and they are a little suspicious of those who do. And I was that way also."

Housewives often mention how they get tired of being asked what they do. "I am a housewife" often gets a look of "That's all?" DaAnna Stringer got tired of feeling that "just because I am a housewife and because I am not doing something that sounds exciting, I get a look like I am a second-class citizen. It's hard work being a housewife, mother and wife. Now, when they ask me, I tell them I am a kept woman—then I watch them shuffle from one foot to the next."

Is your life kept on hold because of the image you are clinging to? Will you feel less of a whole person if you no longer have the title or status position you enjoy?

Of course, not everyone hangs on to a title or a job to build self-worth. For example, some people, like Paul Adams, a 45-year-old bank president, really enjoy their work. "What are some of the ways to substitute for the excitement of business? I like the sense of accomplishment of seeing things happen, employees having a good time. At this point in my life, I would miss the excitement of business challenges."

Would you have the same feeling about your job? Because of the way we have been brought up in our society, it is easier to pigeonhole people by what they do than by who they are—this reinforces our dependency on what we do and the title we carry. It also can make it more difficult to give all this up for a lifestyle change.

WHO CONTROLS YOUR SELF-WORTH?

Have you ever come home from work feeling great, and you get a telephone call from someone who rakes you over the coals? In a five-minute period, you go from feeling great to feeling terrible. Then another call comes in from a friend who was aware of this other person's call, and your friend tells you how great a person you are and not to worry about the earlier call. So now you feel better. You go through a roller coaster of feelings in a 30-minute period.

This situation can give you emotional whiplash. The extent of your injury will depend upon your belief in yourself—your self-worth. If your self-worth is heavily dependent upon the reactions of others, those telephone calls will be going through your mind for the rest of the evening—right into the wee hours of the morning. If your self-worth is strong, you will hear what was said, evaluate it, acknowledge who you are and be accountable for your feelings.

Janet Miller, a 37-year-old hairdresser who opened up her own beauty shop, heartily agreed. "No one can make us happy but ourselves. I can't depend upon anyone but me—that has been a recent helpful revelation."

If your self-worth is dependent on what others say, it is going to be difficult for you to make a lifestyle change, because one moment someone will be praising you for having the courage to try it and the next someone else will be questioning your motives. You will swing back and forth, your emotions gyrating with each swing.

When your self-worth is dependent on others, it affects your decision making. When you receive positive remarks from others, you feel more confident in trying something new. When you get negative input, it threatens your confidence in making a decision. You may know people who flop back and forth when making decisions. Their self-worth and confidence are taking the same swings.

Sometimes we are in a trying relationship or job that gives us constant negative input and finally, over a long period of time, wears us down. This was experienced by Yarnell, a 47-year-old from New York.

Yarnell's self-worth was badly shaken when he got caught in the middle of a departmental reorganization. After 19 successful years, including being awarded several major trips recognizing his management ability, he now had a new boss who was destroying him emotionally:

"My feelings of self-worth went to the cellar. I felt like my humanness was taken away. I didn't feel like a contributor. I didn't want to go to meetings; I didn't want to participate. I had never felt this way before.

"It was hard for me to share my feelings because it involved my ego. You can read all those stories you want to about things that have happened to other people, like in this book you are writing, but when it happens to you it is different. It is really at the gut level then. You don't want to talk to people; you may not even want to be around your friends."

Yarnell went through an emotional hell that could have destroyed him along with his already-devastated self-worth. Fortunately, rather than giving in to his depression, he attacked it head-on.

"When I got to thinking about why someone might want to commit suicide, I thought, Holy Toledo, it's time I talk to a counselor. I had resisted before—I had this feeling I was less of a man if I went. I didn't realize how bad off I was until now."

To help himself rebuild emotionally, Yarnell went to see a counselor—a step that some people may not take willingly. Yarnell's rebuilding process has included taking a spiritual look at life in general. "Through my reading I was reminded that we are unique and we are made in God's image and we are good and whatever another person lays on us is not important."

Yarnell went from having his self-worth beaten down to emerging with greater confidence in being able to handle other challenges. He better understands his own ability to weather storms and knows where to turn to find tools to help. The blinders have been removed. Have you ever gone through a similar humiliation of your self-worth?

If you are going through an emotional struggle like Yarnell faced, don't be surprised if you are unable to think clearly about making a lifestyle change. It's difficult when you can't see the light at the end of the tunnel and you don't even know where you are in the tunnel. Your energy is being absorbed by trying to maintain your sanity and self-worth. It's at times like these that you need to put your life in neutral until you can clear up your thinking. After having a chance to rebuild emotionally, decide what your next step will be.

If you make a lifestyle change, what do you think people will think? Can your self-worth handle it? When I made my change I wondered what people might think. Would they think I couldn't handle the business pressures in a big city? Would they think I was going through a mid-life crisis? Was I running away from something? The reality is that most people are so busy dealing with their own problems, they really don't care what you do. Your close friends will care, but they will also accept whatever you do as being good for you.

Typically when people go to the trouble to roast you, their lives are so boring, roasting you is the most exciting thing to do. Or perhaps they are envious. Either way, they are the ones wasting their energy when they decide to put labels on your behavior, such as jumping around, carefree, unsettled or going through a midlife crisis.

My friend Del Rogers is a very successful businessman, as well as a good counselor. I asked him how he would separate a person going through a so-called midlife crisis from a person who just wanted to make a lifestyle change. Del replied, "I am not sure I would be concerned about the difference. I would say that if a midlife crisis moved them to the point of doing something positive with the rest of their life, that's great."

Society has a way of labeling behavior in easy-to-swallow capsules—especially behavior that is outside the norm. You may remember when there was the big stir about women working. A mother's place was in the home. Although women working outside the home are now commonplace, those who paved the way had to emotionally handle the labels thrown at them. Those labels were aimed right at their self-worth.

When I was fired back in the early 1970s, I kept worrying about what others would say if they knew. Nothing like this had ever happened to me before. My mind was running wild with labels—failure, dumb, no good. My self-worth couldn't face admitting the truth to others. I decided to use the excuse that I was going to go into business for myself and therefore had quit. After I told it enough times it even began feeling like it was the whole truth. In fact it was a partial truth because I had always wanted to start my own business.

Now, 15 years later, I finally have been able to admit to others that I was fired. Some of my friends will find it out for the first time when they read this book—as did my dad when I was discussing writing this book with him.

I distinctly remember sitting around the kitchen table after Sunday dinner and telling our 23- and 20-year-old sons. They both were very surprised. I sat there wondering what they were going to think of their dad. Would I now be a failure in their eyes? Or would my honesty give them strength at some traumatic point in their lives, knowing that things had worked out well for me?

My wife was very understanding. Yet I was concerned that she might feel I was less of a person than she thought. My family could have been very threatening to my self-worth if they had so chosen. I feel very fortunate, for I have spoken with other men who have been fired, whose families made them feel worse. Their self-worth took such a dive that it was difficult to communicate with their families. They felt they had nothing to offer them. With that depressed attitude it is difficult to see the options life has—and we remain stuck on hold. Some people even commit suicide.

Cousin Leroy Dreier, a farmer, told of how farmers need support from their families during today's trying times. "It's tough when you lose the family farm. They think, here I have lost the family farm after all these generations of farmers. One farmer's wife from Iowa was interviewed and she told how her husband's dad had ridiculed him because he had lost the farm. Her husband hung himself in the barn. She felt the ridicule had pushed him over the edge."

Self-worth is very delicate. How people feel about themselves can fluctuate significantly due to input from others. It takes strong self-worth to have the drive to move ahead with your life. It is important for you to take stock of how many of your actions are based on what other people will think and how many are based on what you want to do. Are you living a life built on what you think of yourself or on what you think other people think of you? How is that affecting your thinking about making a lifestyle change?

YOUR VALUES—OTHER'S VALUES

Our values play an important part in the direction we take in our lives. Many of the values we hold on to are values that have been passed down from our parents and teachers. Sometimes these values are so ingrained in our thinking, the thought of doing something else almost seems like heresy.

In making a lifestyle change, you may hear some of your values bouncing around in your head. I did. When you were growing up, for example, were you told the importance of staying at one job and living at one place if you were going to be seen as a stable person? I was.

I remember hearing my parents talking about people who couldn't stick to anything. They were people who jumped from one job to the next, from one city to the next. When I thought about making a lifestyle change and moving from the high-speed world of Dallas to the laid-back setting of Breckenridge, I wondered if that would be regarded as jumping around. Dad's brother Nelson reiterated the family values. "If I see a person jumping from one thing to another, I think the guy is messed up because he doesn't know what he wants."

My dad has lived 74 years within a four-mile radius of where he was born. He was in farming for 43 years, then manufacturing for 21. He didn't need to move from one state to the next to have quality living. My family can't understand why I don't want to move back to Hesston, Kansas. They have lived in that area all their lives and are content. But I am different.

David Winner, 33, told me how surprised his family was when he left Boston after having a very successful hairdressing business there for the past 12 years. "I was ready for a different pace and scenery. My family couldn't understand why I left. They all have lived in the same little area since the Civil War."

Diane Blessing's relatives thought she was crazy when she gave up the security of a high-paying job at age 37. Diane recognized why they felt that way. "These relatives had gone through the Depression, and job security was very important. They couldn't understand how I could give it all up. The older relatives felt it was more important to have a family and a house—rather than a new lifestyle."

When making a lifestyle change, you will be dealing with your values plus other values projected on you from friends and family. There will be people who will congratulate you for making a change and there will be others who will question your sanity. This latter group will cause you to start doubting your own judgment if you haven't carefully worked through your own priorities and values.

"Values go all the way back to childhood," said psychotherapist Bob Hendrix. "When you talk about change, you may be asking people to change their values. If you have a five-generation family in a small town in the Midwest, you have a lot of well-established values. As a person gets ready to make a change, everyone will be standing around broadcasting their values—like 'Why are you going over there?' 'That's a dumb thing to do.' 'You are not going to like it.'"

When Dean and Jean Gray moved from Elgin, Illinois, to where their son lives, one friend remarked, "My son wanted us to move out west near him also, but I wouldn't do that to him and interfere with his life." This comment left Jean with a funny feeling until she worked through the fact that their son was excited about their coming. Some sons might think their parents were too close even if they were clear across the country.

Because people's values are so important to them, they are quick to pass them on to you. A common frustration experienced by those contemplating a change is that many of their friends are happy with the two kids, two cars and a dog existence, and don't understand why anyone would want to make a lifestyle change. Regardless of what you do in your life, you are going to have some friends who think it's great and others who think you have gone off the deep end. The important thing is for you to think through how *you* feel.

Chris Litsey has experienced the importance of tuning in to himself. "It is like back when you were a child and you learn to walk by taking the first step—letting go. Our focus is so intense on impressing other people, we don't stop to listen to what we would like to do. Most of us have many things we would like to do rather than what we are doing, but we don't do them because of what people might think. It is important to let go and pursue what we want to do even if it might look radical to others. Inside you know what will make you happy."

In thinking through making a lifestyle change, it's helpful to talk with someone who has actually made a change—someone who knows how it feels, understands the fears, uncertainties, excitement. If you were thinking about getting married, would you go to someone who is a confirmed bachelor or an old maid, or would you go to someone who is happily married?

Recognize that your own values will continue to change with time. Some of the most obvious changes I have experienced during my lifetime are related to dress codes and eating habits. I remember hearing my mother tell my sister, Alma, that it was not ladylike to wear slacks—especially not to church. Look how that has changed over the years.

Or take eating habits. As a young kid, I couldn't have my desert until I cleaned up my plate—and that included all the fat from the meat. Have you cut things out of your diet that you had to eat as a kid?

Another value shift I experienced was concerning dancing. When I was growing up, dancing was considered a sin. Grandpa Dreier called it "belly rubbing." If you danced you were going to Hell. I remember dancing for the first time when I was 17 and thought, "I'll take my chances." When driving back home that night, I expected lightning to strike me.

What values have you seen change during your lifetime? Are any of these changes affecting your decision to make a lifestyle change?

Another value shift affected by change in my life was a greater focus on the quality of life rather than just accumulating more and more. Growing up poor, I suspected that money was the road to happiness. That's not so. I find more of my happy memories are associated with family, meeting new challenges or helping others—like three years spent volunteering in Africa. Since making my lifestyle change, I have had more time to think through my values and how they have changed. I have learned to evaluate which values are mine and which are society's.

Howard, 48, found the same to be true for him. Howard resigned as the president of a major corporation and now is actively involved in helping to establish mental health and drug abuse centers. "Since the change, I have experienced a much freer way to look at what is out there in life and in my value system than when I was caught up in a daily routine of just meeting business crisis after business crisis."

Your values are the behind-the-scenes guidelines for your life. It is easy to get your values confused with others' values and end up with very mixed emotions. When you make a lifestyle change, you are taking responsibility for your life in a very special way. It's important that the change is in harmony with your values.

Your change is not going to please everyone. If you try to please others you will remain stuck. While others' values are good for them, their values can be a roadblock for you. Perhaps you have already experienced this in your life. Remember, what happens in your life is up to you. You are the one in charge of your life which is directed by your dreams, your drives and your values.

BUILDING SELF-WORTH AND CONFIDENCE

The stronger your self-worth and confidence, the easier it will be for you to make a lifestyle change. It will be easier for you to see your options. You will be able to be more your own person— less dependent on others and what they have to say. You will be better able to overcome the fears and uncertainties that keep others on hold.

To build this mental muscle, you need to feed it. The kind of food you are prepared to accept for your mind will depend on how you see yourself. If you see yourself as being strong, you will accept strong food. If you feel insecure, you will turn away the strong food until you are willing to open up and give yourself a chance.

For the purpose of illustration, give your self-worth a rating between one and 10. A 10 could be compared to a person having the strongest self-worth you know. A one would be a painfully shy person. Lets say you give yourself a six rating.

Let's compare that six rating to a No. 6 screen that my dad used to use to sift wheat. When he wanted only a certain size wheat, he would run the wheat through a sifter and the wheat of that size or smaller would go into the container. The larger wheat would pass over.

We also have sifters in our minds. We have decided what we collect and what we will pass on by. If you have a No. 6 screen in your mind, it will keep out the higher seven, eight, nine, and 10 inputs. If someone gave you a No. 10 compliment like, "You have more talent than anyone I have ever met," you would not hear it; it would pass right over you because it doesn't fit the image you have of yourself.

Meanwhile, if a No. 3 comment like, "Because of your limited talent, we will probably only call on you when we are shorthanded," you would hear it. In order to build your self-worth muscle, you need to hear the strong No. 10 comments.

Sometimes accepting positive comments is like exercising. When I need the exercise the most, I feel least like doing it. I can think of a variety of reasons why I think I can get by without doing if for another day—it's too hot, it's too cold, it looks like rain . . . you can add the others. Likewise, when I need positive inputs the most, I am least ready to accept them. Have you also found this to be true?

When he was in his early 40s, Bob Heath sold his tire store. In the early stages, Bob questioned whether he could do anything but run a tire store. Linda, his wife, had the answer: "I said, 'Bob you can do anything in the world you want to. For heaven's sake, there is no way you can doubt that you can pick up and do anything you choose to do.'"

"That helped me more than anything else," Bob said. "Honestly, when people are in one job for a long time, the thought of trying anything else can be scary. When I decided to go into real estate and go to school to get my license, I loved it. I discovered I could do something else and ended up being the most successful agent they had. This built my confidence. By golly, I can do anything. If I had stayed in the tire business another six or seven years, I might have just doubted myself too much. I definitely have more confidence now than before the move.

"The reason I think people often stay stuck in a rut and don't change is because they don't have enough confidence. However, if you talk to them they will tell you how much confidence they have in themselves. I would tell you how great a store manager I was, but deep down inside I was afraid that I couldn't do other things. I don't think people have the confidence to say, 'I am going to change my life and make a move.' I think that one thing that doesn't occur to people is that there may be a better quality of life someplace else. They go around with little frowns on their faces and never realize there is a better way to live."

Have you ever talked a good story about what you could do, while deep inside you were shaking? How did it feel when you finally admitted you were scared? That's a hard step to take. Yet when you do, people tend to encourage you just as Linda encouraged Bob.

When Karen and I got ready to make our lifestyle change, there were moments when I wondered if we were doing the right thing. Discussions with friends helped me to sort out my feelings. With them I was able to be honest about my feelings of uncertainty. Then I realized the decision felt right. I was ready to slow down the pace and get away from those things that keep a person's day in a whirlwind.

My friend Del Rogers reminded me of the uncertainty I had expressed back in 1971 when I started my business. Because I was able to handle what came along then, he felt I could do it again.

Del's comments got me thinking about the days when I first started calling on businesses to see if they were interested in my seminars. There were days that I would come home with my tail dragging. Every time someone told me "no," I wondered whether it was because they didn't think my seminars were any good or because I wasn't a good salesman. Since I was the salesman and the product, it was a double-whammy. I had just been fired from my last job. What if I couldn't make it in my own business either? I needed something to build my self-worth.

That's when I discovered the importance of feeding my mind with positive input. I had read how our subconscious mind works 24 hours a day and how important it is that we watch what we put in our mind. If we plant a weed, that is what will grow in our mind. If we plant a flower, a flower will grow.

During those days there were a lot of weeds planted when prospective clients would say, "No, come back and see us when you have a little more experience."

To offset the weeds, every night before going to sleep I read a little from each of three books—the Bible, *The Power of Positive Thinking* and *Psycho-Cybernetics*. I would read until I felt good about myself. It was like refueling my engine for the next day. I certainly didn't want to go to sleep with a bed of weeds growing in my mind. Rather, I visualized the growth of all the good thoughts from what I had read. I usually woke up feeling pretty positive about the next day. Admittedly, at times I had to plant another flower to choke out the persistent weeds.

Have you ever experienced the feeling that negative weeds were growing in your mind? Positive input can choke out those weeds. Sometimes it takes several positive thoughts to smother one weed. If you are a gardener, you know how persistent those pesky weeds can be. The key is to keep seeding your mind with positive inputs.

Bill and Myrna Ebert, in their early 50s, discovered the value of positive input from self-development motivational tapes.

"The more we thought about our lives, it became real clear to us that we had to change ourselves. We suddenly started hearing about being your own person, making your own decisions and taking responsibility for those decisions. We started gobbling up tapes, motivation, self-building. We benefitted greatly from it. We could put it into our lives.

"We look back and see where we had been cowards, where we had missed the boat here and there—and we understand why. We just weren't willing to step out and take a risk—we weren't willing to be responsible. We both lacked confidence in what we could make happen—we were in a trap.

"After making our lifestyle change, we had some resentment that we hadn't heard some life-changing messages earlier. Maybe we did and we weren't ready to listen. You get involved in working for the corporation and you don't look up or take time to really listen. We had made overtures during the years but we weren't serious about it. It probably had a lot to do with self-confidence—the ability to move out and say, I am not worried; I can do it no matter what it takes."

One of the rewards I get from giving motivational talks is seeing people start doing things with their lives that they had just talked about before. It's like a gentle nudge. Once they are going, they are often surprised by what they can do.

On the ski slopes, I see those gentle nudges as ski instructors motivate their white-knuckled students. One day I saw a man in his mid-50s learning how to stop by snowplowing. As he slowly started down the gentle slope, the instructor enthusiastically shouted, "That's right. You are doing great. Good, good." Her encouragement brought a look of relief to his tense, hunched body.

The next day I saw the same instructor up the mountain on a much steeper slope with a boy who looked to be around 6 years old. She was showing him how to make smooth turns like you see on TV. As she skied alongside him she encouraged him to relax, bend his knees, shift his weight. When they stopped, I heard her praise him on how great he was doing.

Every time I'm on the mountain, I pass ski instructors giving their students pep talks. It's obvious the instructors know the power of positive input for building confidence. I know that in my case, if the instructor said what he really thought, I might have left the mountain. Positive input made me keep trying one more time.

When was the last time you had a gentle nudge that kept you from giving up? Were you glad someone gave you that nudge? What kind of nudge do you need right now to help you to make your lifestyle change?

When you were growing up, did you get the feeling you could do anything? What was said that gave you that feeling? How do you see those early childhood inputs helping you get more out of life now? Are there any sayings that your parents told you over and over again that still come to mind in times of pressure? How about, "If at first you don't succeed, try, try again." Or, "If it's been done once, it can be done again."

One of my favorites is "I think I can, I think I can," from *The Little Engine That Could.* My mother read that book to me over and over. I remember hearing it one day when I came in hot, thirsty and tired and didn't want to finish mowing the lawn. When I was 5, that yard seemed like acres. When I went back home to take another look as a 48-year-old, the yard appeared to have shrunk. Even though I heard that story over and over, it always made me feel pepped up. So back to mowing I would go—same hot Kansas sun, same twigs jamming the blades. The difference was my improved attitude.

We need positive input to help us move ahead. It may be input from others, spiritual input, books and tapes. You know, or will soon discover, what works for you. Our minds can get stuck just like our cars do. Back on the farm my family would carry a shovel in the car in case we got stuck. Dad would throw sand under the tires from the piles beside the road left by the grader. Despite the frustration of being stuck, Dad would use this time for an object lesson—namely, you will just spin your wheels in life if there isn't anything solid for the wheels to grab.

Your life may be on hold because you haven't put any new thoughts in your mind for your wheels to grab. In the two weeks before you read this book, what new input did you put in your mind to help you from spinning your wheels?

Strength sometimes comes from just taking quiet time for yourself. I make a point of spending at least 30 minutes a day to mentally relax. It's a time when I am away from everyone, with no radio on, no TV—just pure quiet.

Yarnell also realized the importance of quiet times when he was trying to rebuild his self-worth that his boss was destroying. "Something that came through loud and clear in my process of getting through my depression was the value of the quiet sessions that many recommend you take for yourself —just a few minutes each day. It works! It absolutely works! We get so caught up in everyday things we lose sight of the big picture. Those short times helped me feel good about myself."

When was the last time you took that quiet time for yourself? Quiet time is a good time to just let your mind relax and float around thinking about your worth and your life. You will be surprised by the fresh insights you will get from just allowing yourself to spend time with your inner world.

CHALLENGES ARE A RESET BUTTON FOR CONFIDENCE

Judy Andrews has experienced the fearful feeling of having her back against the wall and then coming out with greater personal strength. After months of trying to patch a deteriorating marriage, she encouraged a move from Florida, where she had worked at her parents' marina since she was 12 years old. She hoped the move would bring new life to the marriage. It didn't. Instead, at 31, she found herself in a new community with two small children and lots of feelings of uncertainty.

"I lost 10 pounds; I slept two hours a night. I was sick a lot. I probably could recall every feeling. Now part of me would like to forget those nights when I laid there terrified. The other part of me doesn't want to forget because I feel it is important to remember some of the things you go through so that you can judge the next move.

"The biggest concern was for my two girls, the oldest being in the sixth grade, with all her pre-teenage problems. I bought a business and was putting in 14 to 16 hours a day. It was not easy. I didn't think it was going to be easy. But if I would have realized what I was biting off, I would probably have chickened out. The first season I was concerned financially, emotionally and mentally.

"But . . . Yes, Yes, Yes. I am very glad I did make the move. I hate to think of what I would be doing now if I hadn't made the move. I had a lot of confidence in myself. I had never really had a chance to practice what I felt I could do—until my back was against the wall. Then I had no choice.

"I have discovered the importance of believing in yourself and knowing that you can do whatever you set your mind to do. Then do it. Don't just sit there and talk about it. Don't just sit there and say I can do this—and never do a darn thing. I know too many people like that."

When you are faced with a challenge, it can either build or destroy your confidence. It is not a matter of what happens; rather, it is how you interpret the event. When recapping a painful event in their lives, some people will go into great detail about the pain. They project a feeling of being a "poor me" victim. Do you know anyone like that?

Other people going through the same situation will talk about what they learned and how it helped them later on. Every trial that happens in your life has the potential to build your confidence. As Judy said, she didn't want to forget the past because it helps her judge her next move.

Yarnell came to the conclusion that we have more options than we realize.

"The thing that came so clear to me under my pressure was that we do have options. It sometimes takes counseling or reading to help us see our options—especially when we are down—but we do have options. When you realize that you have options, it gives new hope. There is something to live for.

"Too often we look at life with blinders on. We can only see what is right in front of us, and that may be bleak. When you take the blinders off, you see a lot more."

For Yarnell, a humiliating experience opened up his thinking to other opportunities—opportunities he might not have seen or looked for otherwise. His experience was a reset button for his self-confidence.

Have trying circumstances helped build your confidence or have they reduced it? Have your experiences helped you realize that you have made it in the past and you can make it again? This time you will be smarter and better able to plan your actions with insight. The circumstances in our lives do not make us; they reveal us. As things happen, they tell about us. They tell what kind of internal strengths we have for adjusting to and handling change. These skills are important when taking your life off hold.

HANDLING THE NOW CHALLENGES

Just imagine how your life would be different if you truly believed that you could handle whatever came up. You would no longer have to worry about things that you currently worry about. You would have a new level of confidence that would open doors to doing things you haven't tried before.

Many people are afraid to try something new because of the uncertainties involved. While they may detest their current situation, they hang on to the security of the known. These kinds of attitudes keep people's lives on hold.

As a teenager, I remember the concern I had about the responsibilities of someday being a husband and father. The role seemed mammoth—having to make enough money to support a family. What if the kids got sick? What if I got sick? Fortunately, as I grew older, I became more emotionally prepared to handle those roles. I saw how you just take one thing at a time. After you climb one mountain, you go to the next. You trust your ability to be able to handle situations as they arise.

Any time you talk of change, there is a certain amount of uncertainty that comes along as part of the package. You can look at that uncertainty with excitement and anticipation— like wondering what is going to happen next when reading an exciting novel—or you can look on the uncertainty with heart-pounding fear.

Believe in yourself. Develop a belief that, regardless of what arises, you will be able to handle it one way or another.

The ability to move ahead and handle things as they arise is exemplified by an old college roommate, Marvin Heppner, who recently made a lifestyle change. Marvin, now 49, has tenacity like few have ever seen. In operating his own company he has had one disappointment after another, yet he didn't give up.

Last winter Marvin came up to visit Karen and me in Breckenridge. While he was here, he said that someday he would also like to make a lifestyle change, but would have to pay off his debts first. Besides, his business looked like it might finally be taking off after having struggled with ups and downs for 15 years.

After he got home in January, Marvin wrote, "The time with you and observing your lifestyle caused me to take inventory of my life and think about my goals and future."

Shortly thereafter, he had another serious business setback that knocked the wind out of him like none of the previous had. He began struggling with what he should do. Should he throw in the towel? Should he try it one more time? He knew the business; he had a good reputation in the business. But for some reason, time and time again he had setbacks. He felt like a 50-year-old failure. He was broke. He had just a few pieces of furniture in his little two-bedroom apartment—the rest he had given up in his divorce 10 months earlier. His only claim to success was his two kids, both of whom would make any parent very proud.

This last setback was the "whack on the side of the head" that got him thinking about making a major lifestyle change. He had always loved the Arkansas lakes. He often went there just to get away from business pressures and to have time to think. He thought if he could find some way to make enough money to get by and pay his bills, this might be the time to give it a try. He could still handle his other business clients equally well from Arkansas.

Even though it sounded good, Marvin wondered if he was jumping off the deep end. Was he running away? Or was he running toward something? Was this last business setback a message it was time to make a major lifestyle change? What would his clients say? What would his friend say?

On March 10, Marvin wrote:

"Well—here goes—the biggest change of my life. I will be leaving Dallas 6 a.m. I am moving to Arkansas. In a way I AM EXCITED. In a way I AM FRIGHTENED.

"I am excited about my A-frame house along the lake, which is only costing $200 a month to rent. I am also excited about doing something completely 'off the wall' for me, in that I am going to be a waiter and try to do some yard work around here. I will be trying to take life "one day at a time" and not think of it as such a serious episode as I have been in for almost 50 years. BELIEVE ME, FOR ME THIS IS TRAUMATIC."

I understood how Marvin felt. He was doing something that many want to do but are afraid to try. Many people would never try it if they were in Marvin's financial condition. He was really testing his trust in his ability to handle things as they arise and not worry about the unknowns.

On March 14, he wrote:

"Boy, ya gotta come here—This is great. I've already met some wonderful people, which I feel is an accomplishment since this is only my second day. I will be waiting tables at a nice restaurant with a view that is unsurpassed."

March 21:

"Now that I have done it, I know that it can be done. These people who have a tendency to say,'Well, you know that I can't do that because of my commitments, etc.,' I say 'hogwash.'"

March 28:

"My change is still—and I expect for it to continue to be—very rewarding to me. The people here have other values than in Dallas, in that there is something else in life other than material 'capitalism.' I am focusing on this type of value in life which I have been saying for years that I wanted to do."

April 2:

"I still have some anxieties about this change, but the bottom line is a very strong PLUS. I am trying to take life more in stride, more freely relaxed and go with the flow."

May 1:

"I am more convinced than ever that I made the right decision. My enthusiasm must be showing up over the phone, because my sales have gone up. I love the people I contact at my part-time waiter's job."

Marvin is at the beginning of a new chapter in his life. He has demonstrated that regardless of finances, if you have enough desire and faith in yourself, you can move through the fear of uncertainties. You have trust that you can handle the now moments.

For years I have heard him saying that some day he was going to move to Arkansas. Now he has done it. He is able to make sales for his business from a relaxing setting along the lake, surrounded by flowering trees.

Does that sound like the kind of lifestyle you would like to have? What's keeping you from going for it? Is it because you haven't developed the attitude that you can handle the now challenges? Look at your life. You have been able to handle other uncertainties as they arose. Why do you think you can't do it now? You have more potential than you realize. Just trust it and take your life off hold.

You Can Handle More Than You Expect

People often describe themselves as being frail and not able to handle much. Yet when the pressure is on, there are numerous accounts of people rising to the occasion. Even though you may feel very insecure at times, you have more potential than you ever imagined.

Have you ever had something happen to you that, after it was over, you couldn't believe you had survived? You surprised yourself with the potential you didn't know you had. Just think how your life would be different now if that potential flowed on a daily basis.

People sometimes find this reservoir of potential only after a serious accident. Such was the case with Elaine Fogle as the result of the crash of a small airplane that killed two passengers, including her husband, Ben, and left her partially blind.

"I went through a very emotional time—coming home to where Ben was missing and my lost independence with my blindness. I met with the hospice and they helped me deal with these losses. I went through a time where I had no self-esteem. I hated myself. I did nothing but cry. I hated what I had become. Here I was, a women who couldn't drive a car. I had trouble walking. I couldn't walk down the street from my store to go to lunch. I felt horrible; I was no good. My most-used expression was 'I am sorry.'

"I didn't feel I was worthy to take hospice time from others. The man who was dealing with my case was totally blind and I was sorry that I still had a little sight. I felt guilty that here is a man totally blind and very able to cope with it. I would think, how dare I cry, I have some vision."

Less than two years after the crash Elaine has gotten over those very down moments of feeling so unworthy, but admits she is still making some emotional adjustments. Now, however, she spends more time thinking about the good than the bad. "Generally, when I get down I sit down and mentally list all the good things—my good friends, my home, anything good I will remember. Look at good things, not only bad."

Through her pain, Elaine has experienced a new richness in life, a new appreciation of good friends, a new appreciation of her God.

To meet Elaine today and see her carrying on a successful business, you would never know that at one time she was filled with fear about making the lifestyle change she and Ben made five years before his death.

This lifestyle change came when Ben got fed up with corporate politics and quit his job of 15 years. They moved from the big city life to a small mountain town where they bought their own business—The Balance Sheet. "We decided to go into business for ourselves. If we were going to be faced with corporate politics, it was going to be our own. We took a gutsy cut in pay for the first year, but then our business really took off."

This initial lifestyle change gave Elaine new confidence in her own abilities. But it wasn't until the accident that her true potential came forth:

"At one time in my life, I would have never believed I could come through everything that has happened. We truly set false limitations on ourselves.

"Life is awfully short. My husband was 45 when he was killed. That is a short life. Take the time you have and make it the richest life. You people sitting at the corporate desk: if you hate what you are doing, don't do it. You should love what you are doing. It's not an overnight decision. You have to develop your self-confidence. Ben had it. I didn't. I had to develop it."

Elaine's experience is a testimonial that we can handle more than we ever expect. While we may feel weak and lack confidence in ourselves, we need to trust that within us is an untapped reservoir that is released upon need. Have you ever surprised yourself by being able to handle situations that earlier seemed overwhelming? Do you find that having met the challenge, you now have more confidence? This confidence will help you in making a lifestyle change.

Hilda Wiens, my mother-in-law, made a lifestyle change at age 50 that she wouldn't have thought possible earlier. "After losing my husband in a fatal car wreck, I was forced to do things I never thought I could. This may sound selfish, but if this hadn't happened I would have never discovered what I can do. After Bert was killed 21 years ago, I went back to college at the age of 50 to get my teaching degree."

What are you putting off because you feel you're too old to start?

During trying times, the important thing is being able to get through them without giving up. It is like exercising. It takes a commitment to not give up. It is easy to start feeling sorry for ourselves and never experience our true potential.

While we often discover what we are made of during trying times, it is easy to fall into a trap instead. Rather than rising to the occasion, we spend our time bemoaning what happened to us. Elaine and Hilda moved ahead with their lives and now have grown from it. Other people find it hard to move ahead, and so they remain stuck in bad feelings.

It is easy to get bogged down with bad feelings unless you look at the good, as Psychotherapist Ken Unruh found:

"People get very stuck on feeling bad. My task is to help them experience good. After they have shared their problem, I look at them and say this may be one of the biggest opportunities of their life. They often want to hit me when I say that. Pain and anguish are opportunities for personal growth. People have the answers within themselves, but when they are torn and feeling bad about themselves, they can't capitalize on their own resources. A counselor can help them get in touch with their resources.

"People who adjust to change have a basic strong sense of self. Accordingly, they have faith that things will work out for them even though they can't see it or touch it at the moment. They have an attitude of adventure and reaching for life. They are on the offensive rather than the defensive. It is a whole mode of operation of attacking rather than being fearful of life."

Would you describe yourself as being fearful of life, or are you attacking it with confidence? If you are not attacking life with confidence, what do you plan to start doing to build up your confidence? Don't wait for something traumatic to happen that will force you to release your potential. Do it now.

ACTION BUILDS CONFIDENCE AND SELF-WORTH

It is easy to read and philosophize about building self-confidence, but nothing happens until you start doing something. Just reading about building confidence and doing nothing would be like reading about the value of exercising, but never getting out of your chair. You have to do something.

You may remember when you first learned to ride a bicycle. You probably had someone telling you how to do it, but it wasn't until you got on the bike that you really started getting a feeling of what it was like.

When I was 5, my Dad bought me a bike after much coaxing. After further coaxing, he took time after the evening chores to help me learn to ride it. It looked real simple—until I tried it.

The gentle slope of our dirt lane looked perfect for learning. Awkwardly getting on the big bike, I started rolling down the lane. Faster and faster I went until I hit a little rut and fell over. It seemed so fast and I felt so high in the air. It was an entirely different experience being on the bike than it was watching someone else ride. All the things I had to remember—pedal backward to use the brakes, lean this way, lean that way.

When I got going fast, I forgot it all. But little by little it became easier as my confidence grew.

Experiences like this helped me realize the importance of doing and not just thinking about doing. The first time I gave a speech to a large audience, I was scared to death. My stomach was churning, my voice quivering, my knees shaking. My body was an emotional wreck. But after doing it, I was better prepared to do the next one. My confidence grew with each speech.

There are all kinds of books on giving speeches, but nothing beats getting in front of an audience. When you are standing up there with your heart pounding in your ears and your stomach churning, it's different from just reading about it in a book. Wouldn't you agree?

Can you remember reading something that seemed simple until you actually tried it and got the full impact of what was being described? What did you learn by doing it that you never would have learned by just reading about it? How did actually doing it affect your self-confidence? Do you have more confidence now than you did before trying? The same thing is true when making a lifestyle change.

Next time you have a challenge you are tempted to walk away from, stick with it. You don't build confidence by walking away. Your self-worth will increase each time you successfully accomplish something you were afraid of before. There will be times that you will "fall off the bicycle," but don't let that stop you from trying it again.

Doing little things step by step helps build confidence—even in social settings. Shirley, 37, described herself as a shy computer programmer who would only talk to people she knew when she was at parties. "I decided that if I was going to stretch myself, I had to visit with strangers. At first it was really scary for me, but after doing it at several parties, my circle of acquaintances started growing and I now get invited to more parties than ever. I feel much more comfortable around strangers and it has even helped me in my work."

In social settings do you normally talk with people you know or do you reach out for strangers? When you go to a meeting do you sit next to strangers or near people you know? At my seminars, I usually find people sitting down with the people they know. Familiar faces are like a security blanket. Next time you have the choice of sitting beside a stranger or someone you know, stretch yourself. Sit by the stranger—you may develop a new friend.

As you reach out and stretch, you will be building the muscle of your self-confidence. You will build the strength that will help you take your life off hold. As you take your life off hold and move forward, you will be improving your quality of life.

SUMMARY: THOUGHTS ON TAKING YOUR LIFE OFF HOLD

Your self-worth is like a muscle that propels you through life, giving you more self-confidence with each success. All people have areas of their lives in which they wish they had more confidence. What is yours? The good news is that there are ways we can build our confidence.

While there are times that we were short-changed when it came to getting our fair share of confidence, I have never heard of a doctor announcing to a new mother that she has just given birth to a confident child. Admittedly, some children receive more positive input in their young years than others. That can affect their confidence level. We all have things we wished we had learned when we were younger that would help us be more confident now—but that was then and now is now. We move on from here.

Have you ever held a baby chick? Growing up on a farm, I used to love picking them up and brushing their soft feathers against my face. They were like little yellow balls. They were so cute it was tempting to squeeze them. Dad had to remind me that if I held the chicks too tightly, I might kill them. It was better to let them go and grow.

The same is true with your life. You can squeeze it so tight that you kill it. Instead, let it spread its wings. Every time you turn away from trying something new, you are keeping your life on hold. The tighter you squeeze the security blanket, the more it slows down your growth.

Have the courage to go for it. You may fail the first time, but that doesn't make you a failure. Rather, it makes you smarter. You now know what to do differently next time.

People with strong self-worth use their trials and disappointments to help them grow stronger. As they put the pieces of their lives back together, they have strength to move ahead. Quite a contrast from people who rot away in front of the TV.

Time and time again, people have found they can handle more than they ever expected. They look back after a traumatic event and say how surprised they are that they were able to handle it. Having made it, they now have a new sense of personal strength for what lies ahead.

Is your self-worth dependent on your job title or the size of your checking account? If so, this can be a roadblock to your making a lifestyle change unless you are willing to adjust your thinking. The stronger your self-worth, the less threatened you will feel by giving up a prestigious title or job.

You probably know someone whose whole life is their job. When Barbara Walters interviewed Bud McFarland after his suicide attempt, she asked him how he looked at life differently now. "I learned you should not judge your worth by your work," he said. Some people would feel like an empty shell if it weren't for their work. If they fail at something, they consider themselves worthless.

People with this frame of mind have a particularly hard time adjusting to retirement. All of a sudden they don't have a place to go in the morning. They don't have a title or people relying on them. While retirement sounded appealing at first, they are now faced with a lonely, drifting feeling.

Lifestyle changes include a number of uncertainties. You can systematically tackle them one at a time or do nothing. Doing nothing is not an option if you want to live a full life.

People across America go to work every day complaining all the way, yet they don't have the confidence to move off dead center. They don't realize the potential they have for making things happen. They feel they are victims of circumstances, the boss, society or whatever else they choose to blame.

Don't get caught in the trap of thinking, if I had as much confidence as so-and-so, then I wouldn't be afraid. It is easy to do nothing if you start comparing yourself with others. Many people have talked themselves out of making lifestyle changes because someone else had been afraid to try it.

How much of your thinking is influenced by what happens to others? If you get a raise and someone else gets a bigger one, does that take away the good feelings about your raise? Do you compare your level of confidence with that of others? Why? What do you think you gain through this comparison? What do you lose?

When you spend your time playing these comparison games, you take away time and energy from developing your confidence. Spend this time on more positive activities such as reading self-help books or listening to motivational tapes. Confidence and self-worth can help you move your life off hold. It is up to you.

QUESTIONS AND ACTIVITIES TO HELP BUILD YOUR SELF-CONFIDENCE

The following activities and questions are designed to help you follow through on the ideas in this chapter. You may find some of them more helpful to you than others, depending on your background.

1. Make a list of five things you feel very confident in doing. How did you develop this confidence?

2. How would gaining confidence in those five areas help you to gain confidence when making a lifestyle change?

3. Who do you admire for their self-confidence? How do you know they are really as confident as you think they are? What lessons can you learn from them?

4. List five things that you are afraid to try, and why. What would have to change before you would be willing to tackle them?

5. What were the three most valuable points you got out of this chapter? Why were they the most valuable for you? What does that tell about you?

6. Look at the forces of change that you diagrammed in the last chapter. If your self-confidence or self-worth were 10 percent higher, how would it affect each of these pushing or

retarding forces?

7. What things have happened in your life that have most helped you to build your confidence?

8. Write down your ideal lifestyle change. In what areas do you need confidence to feel more comfortable about moving ahead? What are you going to do to get that confidence?

9. Develop a program that will feed your mind with positive thoughts before you go to bed. Motivational books or tapes are most helpful.

10. Does your morning routine give your day a strong base to work from or is it hit and miss? Develop a program that involves a little quiet time to feed your mind with positive thoughts. Get up 30 minutes earlier and begin your day with a brisk 20-minute walk so you can spend time thinking about your life. Think how lucky you are and how glad you are to be alive. Feed your mind with good positive thinking. Plant flowers, not weeds. When you come home, spend 10 minutes reading or listening to tapes to further feed your mind with positive inputs. Try this for 30 days. You will be surprised at the difference it will make in your ability to tackle each day's challenges.

11. Keep a journal of the things that happen during the next month to build your self-worth and to set it back.

12. If your mind is cluttered because you are upset with someone, build your confidence by going to talk with that person. Begin by saying you feel the communication has broken down between the two of you and you are wondering what you did that caused that to happen. Even though you may feel it is the other person's fault, have enough personal self-worth to listen instead of jumping on them. You want to open up communication, not prove someone is right or wrong.

JONES-PHOBIA

THE FEAR OF NOT KEEPING UP

If you have been struggling with the thought of making a lifestyle change but can't get off dead center, Jones-phobia may be the culprit that is keeping you stuck. The effect of Jones-phobia slowly creeps up over a period of time. It stems from the belief that more is better, that material possessions can make you happy. That belief is the driving force behind the fear of not keeping up—with the Joneses.

I have found that people struggling with change do not realize the grip that Jones-phobia has on their lives. They need to look at their beliefs. Is your happiness tied up in what you own? Is your self-image tied up in what you own? Do you believe that salt makes things sweet?

Once upon a time a remote village was searching for the secret of how to make food sweeter. The village people had tried everything. One day a salesman came to the village with a secret ingredient called salt. The salesman told the villagers that salt would make their food sweeter. He was very smooth and convincing and finally the village people started using salt believing it would make their food sweet.

Some said, "Oh yes, salt definitely makes my food sweeter." Those who disagreed were told to add more salt.

And so, the village people began to work very hard to get more salt. The more salt they had, the more successful they were thought to be by the other villagers.

One day another visitor came to the village and said, "Salt doesn't make food sweet." Arguments broke out among the villagers. Some said, "Yes it does," and others said, "No it doesn't." Confusion spread.

The wise old village chief stepped forward and said, "If you believe salt makes food sweeter, then so shall it be for you. If you believe that salt does not make food sweeter, so shall it be for you. Believe what you believe, not what others believe. And remember, if things aren't tasting the way you want, then you need to re-examine your beliefs."

YOUR BELIEFS—QUANTITY OR QUALITY?

Do you believe that salt makes things sweet? Do you believe that money makes people happy? Do you believe that more is better—having for having's sake? Your beliefs can significantly affect how you spend your time and what you do with the rest of your life. As you believe, so goes your life. If your life is not working for you, it's time to re-examine your beliefs.

Are you afraid that life will be boring without material possessions? Think about what happens when you stop using salt. Food tastes bland at first—and then you get used to it.

There is a prominent belief in our society that more is better. This belief is rooted in our early childhood experiences. We wanted more marbles; we wanted more toys; we wanted more candy. When we wanted more cake and got it, we discovered that more can sometimes make us sick. That should have told us something.

Why shouldn't we think that more is better? Why shouldn't we believe that material things can bring happiness? We are constantly bombarded with ads telling us what to buy and drink and wear if we want to have the full life. "You can have it all," the ads promise. If you kept hearing that salt made things sweet, you would probably end up believing that it does.

Little by little our beliefs become integrated into our value system. Everyday decisions are affected—decisions that influence what you are going to do with the rest of your life. If your value system is ingrained with the belief that material possessions can make you happy or more successful, it is apt to keep you stuck in a lifestyle that is hard to change. Many people are afraid to make lifestyle changes because they don't want to give up what they have worked so hard for. In a sense, we are like white rats running through the maze of life always hoping that the next turn will hold the reward that will make all this stress and work worthwhile. But there's always another turn.

A recent visitor to this country remarked to me, "It appears the technological revolution has put you people in a cycle where you feel the need to have the latest TV, car, clothes, so you keep working harder to get these purchases. You end up spending a lot more money than it actually takes to live. You are caught in a vicious cycle."

Rolland, a manager for a Fortune 500 company, acknowledged, "I don't care how much you have, you want more and you get caught in a situation—the move toward materialism. It is a drive within you that you get caught in. You want more and more. I have found, if you don't stop and smell the roses, you will never be happy with the money you have."

It is one thing to put in long hours in order to buy basic necessities for survival—food, shelter, clothes—but it is another thing to be attached to a lifestyle predicated on buying from Neiman-Marcus rather than Penney's, and buying Cadillacs instead of Fords. We are not discussing people who stay awake at night worrying about where the next meal is coming from, but rather, people who stay awake trying to decide what kind of coffee grinder to buy, then wonder why they want more out of life.

Survival—Security—Belonging— Self-Esteem—Self-Actualization

Each of us has different needs. Psychologist Abraham Maslow recognized this when he developed his Need Hierarchy. Maslow was interested in finding out what motivated people to work, what pushed their hot button. He discovered that people are motivated by unsatisfied needs. The hierarchy of those needs is represented in this triangle.

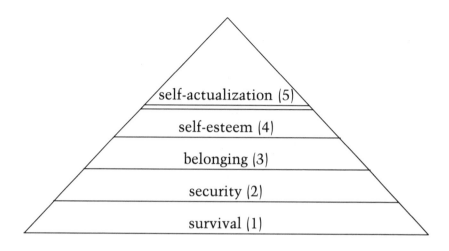

We begin with the most basic need of survival—food, clothing and shelter. When that need is mostly satisfied, we become more interested in satisfying our security needs, such as keeping the job we have so we can continue to survive. After this level of need is mostly satisfied, our interests turn more to having a feeling of belonging. We want to be a part of the group. We want to be loved. People buy certain kinds of clothes because they make them feel part of the "in" group. This is true of teenagers—as well as those of us with graying hair.

The first two levels of the need hierarchy are concerned with largely physical needs. The third, fourth and fifth are of a more psychological nature. Because of the psychological nature of the top three, it is difficult to say exactly where one stops and the next one begins in our lives.

The fourth level is the need for self-esteem. This is the need to be appreciated as a person, to be valued for who we are and what we have to offer. A person who does a good job as a carpenter or as a singer or as an employee is satisfying that need. Unfortunately, employees often don't feel appreciated by their bosses.

People who buy a one-room house are fulfilling a basic survival need; those who buy a 10-room house have gone beyond basic survival and are motivated by the image the house projects as well as by its comfort.

Self-actualization is the fifth level of Maslow's triangle. People who reach this level are doing their own thing. Typically they are entrepreneurs—people who go into business for themselves, or take on special projects in the community. They break out of material and emotional constraints that can hold us back. The famous Kennedy family, with their active involvement in politics and social issues, is a family that operates largely from the fifth level.

For my management consulting work, I developed a test that helped determine which need levels the employees found to be most important. Test results indicated the majority were concerned about self-esteem and self-actualization. These two levels relate to the quality of life and making the most out of it.

A lot of people belong to the right country clubs and live in the right part of town to satisfy their need for self-esteem and their need to belong to a group. Some people are dismayed when they find material things do not fulfill their needs in these areas. In this chapter, we will be hearing from people who have examined how materialism did or did not help them satisfy these higher-level needs.

Stop for a moment and think where would you put yourself in the hierarchy. Which level is your greatest need level? How are you going about trying to fulfill that need level? Is it working for you or are you frustrated about feeling on hold?

A SALT-FREE DIET

New Beliefs—New Priorities—New Life

"Society has put a lot of pressure on us to succeed in terms of monetary and material success. It becomes a treadmill in and of itself because the more you have, the more you want. You see you haven't quite achieved all those things you were after. You get all the cars you want and you still want more. You want that next condo or that next yacht. The materialistic value system is very subtle and creeps in over a period of a lot of years."

These feelings were expressed by Howard, a former president of an NYSE manufacturing company.

Bob, 37, a successful real estate developer, reflected on how Jones-phobia and status played a large part in his previous business. "I used to buy $1,500 suits, drive a 300 SL Mercedes, live in a 5,000-square-foot house behind a big security wall. It's nice not to have to be caught up in that facade anymore. I don't care if I never have to put my gold cufflinks back on. In our neighborhood, if one neighbor put in a swimming pool, next thing you know, another neighbor would be building a pool plus a tennis court. There was a continuous 'Can you top this?' attitude."

Mary Jane Burgess and her husband, seeing the negative effects of Jones-phobia on their lives, decided to quit their jobs and work as missionaries in Grenada, West Indies, for three years. Two weeks before their departure, Mary Jane reflected on what made them decide to sell everything and head for Grenada:

"I feel it is important to look at priorities. We have always tried to keep our family—three children—as our number one priority. In the last couple years we have had a lot of stress, trying to make another dollar. We have kids in high school and it was keeping them in the best clothes, keeping them in cars, going to the best places for them, keeping them on the dating circuit, keeping them active with their friends, who have a lot of money. It seemed that everything was a matter of keeping up, so a year ago we decided we had enough. We decided to pursue something my husband and I had talked about since we got married. Namely, going overseas and doing mission work.

"A lot of people around here have the 'keeping up with the Joneses attitude' and we were getting caught up in it. We watched families disintegrate for the almighty dollar and we didn't want that.

"Selling everything was tough. I had to make peace with my antiques. I went around and touched each antique and said good-bye to each piece. The rest of the stuff I looked at and said 'So what. It's made out of wood and nails and material, and if I ever need another chair, I can buy one.'

"I have learned the importance of not getting attached to things, but rather getting attached to people. Memories you can take with you wherever you are, and things can always be replaced."

Do you know anyone who acts as if people can be replaced more easily than things? How do you feel when you are around such a person? If you really want to know what a person's belief system is, you don't have to ask. Actions speak louder than words. Just watch what they do with their time. A husband who tells his family that they are the most important thing in his life, yet spends all his free time at the office or on the golf course, is kidding himself or his family.

Are you stuck right now because you are reverently hanging on to some belief that more is better? Have you ever thought that, in some cases, less might be more?

Richard, 45, declared personal bankruptcy after losing $550,000. "As strange as it may seem, I feel more relaxed now that I don't have all those things that I thought would make me happy. I used to spend time trying to figure out how I could afford to buy that new car. Then after I got my new car I spent time worrying about someone parking by it and dinging the door. While I hated to lose everything, I have developed some new values as a result of my bankruptcy which I think will add more depth and quality to the second half of my life."

Have you ever had a trying situation in your life that ended up giving you a fresh new perspective, and from that new perspective your life took on a new richness? While experience can be a ruthless teacher, it can also be a teacher who teaches us lessons that we wouldn't have paid attention to otherwise.

Such was the case with Kathleen Deppner, whose father was killed in a car accident when she was 17. "Since we went through the experience with losing Dad when we did, it has affected the way I have handled my life and makes me realize there are more important things than material things—such as doing things together as a family."

Kathleen's husband, Fred, 43, added, "I think people get hung up in the economic struggle of just keeping up, paying the bills, getting by, being able to buy a little of this and a lot of that. They are so involved in those things of living and working that they don't sit down to think creatively, to think exactly what is going on around them. Meanwhile, the family grows up. I think people need to slow down and get their priorities straight."

Dixie Agnew, a family counselor, related a situation that she referred to as "happening far too often." Both parents were working to keep up the payments on their new house in the better part of town. "The mother bemoaned not having more time with the kids. However, she felt where they were living was a real plus for the kids. The kids said they would rather have their parents more involved in school events and not working all the time. Joy, their high school junior who is on the drill team, related how her friend didn't live in near as nice of a house, didn't have a pool, but their family had so much fun together—going on picnics, hiking and other simple things. The 13-year-old son said he knew his dad had to work hard to be successful, but he wished his dad would at least attend one of his football games this year. He missed them all last year."

When is the last time you sat down to take a careful look at your priorities? Are you afraid to take a look? Has your family grown up while you were at work? What could you have done to have had more time with your family? Is the quantity of your living taking away from quality family time? Are you stuck with a lifestyle that you will look back and hate?

YOUR SELF-WORTH—YOUR MONEY

How would you feel if, like Fred Deppner, your business went from 33 employees to one during the course of a six-month period. What would that do to your self-image?

"I guess if a person took an objective look at my situation, you would say, ' That guy really crashed.' I did go through a period of feeling depressed. Then I stepped back and said, 'I have a lovely wife, a lovely daughter.' I counted the things that were important. While family is important to me, it may not be as important to others. I have always liked challenges, and this is, vocationally, as big a challenge as I have ever faced.

"I am more comfortable with myself today than a year ago mainly because I am not bombarded with a lot of superficial paraphernalia that at the time you think is incredibly important. Now I realize that a lot of stuff was just garbage and what does it mean anyway? It's the darnedest thing I have ever seen. Those things that you thought were so important, that you thought you had to have, after doing some careful thinking, you discover you really don't need them. Sometimes we just buy things to make us feel good about ourselves. I have learned that what is truly important is responding to a challenge and knowing you are good enough to meet the challenge—that is what makes you feel good about yourself—it's not the money."

Why is it that we tie so much of our worth into the material possessions we have accumulated? Have you ever noticed how some people are able to weave into the conversation something about their condo, or their sailboat, or maybe a recent trip to Europe? While it may be of interest, more often it may be a way to remind you who they are—or at least who they want you to think they are. Have you ever done that? So have I.

If your self-worth is tied up with the things you own or the amount of money you make, you are headed for a terrifically depressing time if you should ever have a setback. Such was the case with Tom, from Ohio. I told Tom I wanted to interview him because I had heard he was a very successful businessman.

Tom began the interview telling of his numerous accomplishments when he was in his 20s. He had been nominated as one of the outstanding Men in America, had numerous athletic trophies, had been on the dean's list. After school he went right up the career ladder.

He went fishing in Alaska every year, traveled around the world, had a boat, a couple of condos, a quarter-million-dollar house with a big pool, his wife had a beautiful mink and the list went on. Next year, at 54, he was intending to sell his stock and retire as company president. But then Tom was fired.

"The last 90 days have probably been the most frustrating in my life. I have lain awake every single night since the day I got fired. Right now is a very difficult time for me because I was with the company for 22 years.

"I look like a horse's-rear in my two sons' eyes, which has never been the case before. I was the president of the company. I go in one day and the next day I am on the outside looking in.

"I am worried about how I am going to pay the tuition for my son next week. Early on I decided that I was going to put my children through school. That satisfies my self-image. The one son has come up to me and said, 'Why don't I work for a semester rather than going to school because of the financial problems that you and mom got.' That hurt. That was devastating to me, for him to even have to think of that—coming from where I thought I had gone.

"I have to level with you, Ted. When you came and asked if I would be open to an interview because you had heard I was a successful businessman, I was embarrassed. I don't feel very successful right now. I feel like I have been whipped. Right now I am pretty disgusted when I look in the mirror and see who I see.

"I was so close, I thought, to retiring and now I have to step back and say I have to work for a few more years. I am over 50 years old. I'm no longer a young kid. I don't feel I can go out and just find another job real easily.

"I don't know how to adjust to not having the materialistic drive. I guess I would question my own ability. Money never was a problem and now it is. I am scared for the first time in my life and I am not used to that feeling.

"I don't have my job, but I do have my family. I think of the fellow who woke up when he was 80 years old and found he had bypassed his family. That's sad! When I was having my success, I would forget the family a week at a time because I was working six to seven days a week. Now

I see how strong my family is, which I never slowed down long enough to really appreciate."

Tom had always displayed the all-American image of success. Now for the first time in his life he had to pull back. With so much of his self-worth tied up in money and position, it is difficult for him to get a handle on what to do for the rest of his life.

My prediction is that as Tom grapples with his situation he will look back at these times as being the foundation of some of the richest days in his life. Only time will tell. When I told him that, his comment was, "I hope you are right, but at this time I am a long way from betting on it."

NEW OPTIONS FOR NEW LIFE

Imagine how you would feel if you were in the middle of a traumatic situation and someone suggested that this might be the beginning of some of the richest days in your life. Absurd? You also might think that it was a little naive to think that Tom's frustrating situation has potential richness in it. But when people have their backs against the wall, creativity and options can come to the rescue, providing all their emotional energy isn't spent on the "poor me" syndrome.

As Tom reflects on his potential, he will recognize that he is no longer as energetic as he was as a 21-year-old. But he will also realize he has a compensating balance of experience and savvy from past successes that will help him as he moves to the next chapter of his life. However, it will take a special effort to be positive and objective now that all his props have been knocked out. As Tom works through his dilemma, he will see other options that bring quality to living besides buying mink coats. Most married couples fondly recall how much fun they had the early days of marriage when they didn't have any money. How they made bookshelves from cinderblocks and boards, or tables from wooden boxes covered by sheets.

Tom's situation is an opportunity for the whole family to pull together. An opportunity to share gut feelings. An opportunity to let his two boys know that there are things that happen in life that can make a big man cry—and that's not a weakness. It will be tough at first for the family to explore new options for the future, since all of Tom's earlier dreams were tied in with running a business and making a good profit. In a sense, spending all of one's time thinking about business is like playing one note on the piano. If other notes are added, they can make a harmonious chord—which is much more interesting than a single note.

As you generate more options, it takes away the fear that exists when you are locked into one possibility. People often find themselves on hold because they have become a one-option person—and quite often that option revolves around money. Money, in turn, becomes their measure of well-being. The more money they make, the better they feel about themselves, and the better they feel about themselves, the more money they make. However, the cycle can go both ways—the less money you make, the worse you feel about yourself.

Avoiding a Recipe of Emptiness

Psychotherapist Ken Unruh emphasized, "Money and material belongings are not an indicator of a person's well-being and human spirit. The human spirit is much broader than material assets. People have a remarkable potential to persevere—which has nothing to do with money.

"Money can impede personal growth because there is the deception that money can give fulfillment. Money and titles do not seem to have much to do with fulfillment unless you have developed your own feeling of goodness and experience it on a daily basis. You may obtain wealth, but you will not experience wealth unless you first experience your own goodness. You experience your goodness when you realize that you are a valuable and worthy person in your own right and not based on how many material possessions you have. Trying to build your worthiness through possessions is a recipe for emptiness."

Don felt this emptiness at age 36 when he decided to stop working:

> "When I was in college I kept hearing the professors talking about making the big bucks. I accepted those goals

and pursued them, and between work and wise investments, I have made a lot of money.

"I used to go through the alumni publication of the
university where I got my MBA and look to see what the
average salary of the graduates was. Then I would measure
my salary against that. It was a competitive game that was
consuming my life because I had to spend 14 hours a day,
six days a week to maintain my position. There wasn't
time for anything else.

"When I stopped working, my dominant feeling was
worthlessness. By the criteria of my university and what
I had set for myself, I had been tremendously successful
and now I was no longer in the game. It was a hollow
feeling."

When was the last time you had that hollow feeling? What
caused it? Did it come from what you were thinking about
yourself or from what you thought others might be thinking of
you?

How do you build up your self-image? Is it your prestigious
address, the designer clothes you wear, the car you drive, your
title, the Rolex watch, the big diamond? How would you feel
about yourself if all that changed?

"I feel terrible in admitting this," Janice said, "but when
I don't have my diamond on, a two-carat stone, I feel less important in the grocery line than when I am wearing it. I can see
people out of the corner of my eyes glancing down at my hand.
Makes me feel proud to wear it. I guess that is why ladies wear
mink coats. It makes them feel good about themselves—mink
coats certainly aren't any warmer than much cheaper coats."

An expensive perfume manufacturer admitted that the
difference in cost of making a very expensive perfume and
making a less expensive one is not that great—at least not
nearly as great as the price reflects. The secret to the expensive
perfume is that when you smell it on someone, you know it
cost a lot of money, which suggests success. (If it was a gift, it
suggests the giver is successful or madly in love.)

People go to such extremes to impress others that they
even buy counterfeit symbols of prestige. A Michigan therapist

told of a patient who had just gotten an order of fake Rolex watches, which he was selling for $45 each. While the therapist didn't buy one, the episode did make a good starting place for the therapy session. Interestingly, the patient's dentist had bought a watch.

"We are susceptible to buying things that give us that image. It is hard to maintain the American dream," said an Atlanta therapist. "I have a client who has real financial problems—a touch-and-go situation. He found a good deal on a Mercedes and bought it because it represented the image of the type of person he wanted to be. In knowing him, I can see where his family background influences having this particular need. If he goes down the tube, his ego is blown."

Sally did some strong soul-searching while living in Arizona. After changing to a less demanding lifestyle she could see how much of her ego had been wrapped up in her standard of living. "I used to spend $13,000 a month on the household budget, plus $20,000 a year on clothes. I don't need that now." How much of your ego is dependent on your current lifestyle? This might be a good time to give that some serious thought.

LIVING AN IMAGE FOR OTHERS

Some people have their whole self-image tied up in what other people think of them. Do people think I am successful? Do they think I am smart? Do they think I am pretty or handsome? To a degree, we all have a certain side that we show to other people. We may dress a certain way or say certain things to get someone's attention, but when it becomes an obsession to please or impress other people, then we are no longer in control. Someone else is calling the shots for our life. We are in a rut that keeps us from truly experiencing life to the fullest.

Dependency on other people is referred to as external locus of control. People with an external locus of control tend to be more materialistic. They are more dependent upon other people for their sense of well-being. When they consider making lifestyle changes, you hear a lot of phrases like, "What would our friends think? What would so-and-so think?" When they have a financial setback, not only do they deal with having less money to spend, they also put a lot of emotion into how others are now going to look at them.

Such was the case with Arland, a widower with two young daughters. On first meeting, you couldn't help but notice his expensive jewelry, Rolex watch, name-brand clothing, not to mention the two Mercedes parked in front of his large home. He was a super salesman of oil field supplies. In 1986 he was hit with a 50-percent cut in income because of the drop in oil prices and subsequent slowdown in oil drilling. He couldn't handle lowering his lifestyle, giving up the Merecedes, so he committed suicide. According to most people's standards, he was still rich even with the 50-percent cut. It wasn't a matter that he was poverty stricken; rather, he was emotionally stricken. His whole image was linked with how he thought others saw him.

People with an internal locus of control do not dance to someone else's tune. Rather, they look inside to see how they feel and are able to make decisions less encumbered by other people's opinions.

Sahara, 38, showed an internal locus of control when she made a move from Florida to a different, more relaxed style in Arkansas. "People couldn't believe I was making the move and thought I was crazy for giving up my administrative assistant job plus the beautiful condo. I have had to scale back my living significantly, but I am doing exactly what I want to do. I have learned from experience that no one but me can make me happy. I look at my friends and they are always talking about something they want to buy—and it is usually because another friend has got one. It seems they are living for someone else."

Mrs. Long echoed what Sahara said when she told how her two high-school-age sons reacted differently to living and dressing for others. "Our older son never had to 'keep up with the Joneses.' A shirt was a shirt. He was his own person, while the second son has to wear all the label stuff. If it doesn't have a label in it, he won't wear it. He is very concerned if his hair looks right, if he looks good. I can already see this in the boys. It is going to be interesting to see how this pattern affects them in later life."

Those who have made a change to a simpler lifestyle find that their need to buy label clothing and name brands has diminished. Their values become more internal and less a matter of performing for others. This newfound independent attitude mirrors the independence they showed when making their lifestyle change. You might say they have begun a salt-free diet. No longer caught in the Jones-phobia trap, they need less salt to make life taste good.

Sean Schneider, 34, explained how his priorities have also changed since making a lifestyle change. "I grew up in Toronto and admit that I am a materialistic person. I always bought expensive clothes, Mercedes—lots of nice things. That's not important to me now. I have a $200 Toyota that I wouldn't have been seen in in Toronto—it gets me around. My values have shifted since moving to a slower life pace."

Looking at your own life, how much of your physical and emotional energy is spent on trying to impress someone else? What do you think people would say if you dressed as you really wanted to?

NO ONE LIKES GOING BACKWARD

People normally hate to think of losing ground. They have worked so hard to get where they are, the thought of having to start over is depressing. They often don't feel they have the energy now that they had when they were younger.

"Keeping my nose to the grindstone" is one way of describing my work habits. While that can be good for awhile, if I am not careful, I find myself blindly plugging along. This is an easy way to get in a rut that can affect my thinking.

During a slow time in my business I was putting in 60 to 80 hours a week, week after week. My business associate asked me, "How do you see the business?" I quickly answered, "I see it as a huge stone, one of those big stones like you see cartoon characters pushing up a hill, and I am pushing this stone up this steep mountain."

"That's terrible!" was the response. I had never thought about it being terrible; it just was the way I saw it.

Looking back, it *was* terrible. As I pictured it in my mind if I had slipped as I was pushing the ball up the mountain, the ball would have come rolling back over me. Based on the size of the stone, it might have crushed me. The mountain in my mind did not have a plateau; it was straight uphill. There was no resting. If I had, the ball would have come rolling back down.

When you have thought about making a change in your life, has the fear of losing ground kept you stuck? Or have you thought, "Nothing ventured, nothing gained." How much of what you now cling to are you willing to risk?

George, a 20-year employee for a small manufacturing company, remarked, "I have thought about making a lifestyle change, but I hate to give up what I have gained over these 20 years of work for the same company. It seems like I am finally getting to where I don't have to keep putting in overtime to make ends meet."

George lived in a four-bedroom house in a nice middle-class part of town. He had a swimming pool and an inboard motorboat. He enjoyed going out to the lake on weekends with friends. Once a week he played racquetball at the local sports club. His wife drove a two-year-old Buick and he had a year-old Honda. One-fourth of the clothes he and his wife wore were name brand; the rest were a mixture of middle-of-the-road lines.

"It is hard for me to give up anything," George said. "I have worked so hard for what I have. I know I don't need to have a boat, for a lot of people don't have boats, but we have had such good times on the boat. I guess we could move to a smaller place without a pool but we have waited so long to have a place with a pool."

George obviously was not ready to give up anything in order to make a change. He had an itch to do something different but at the same time he wanted to hang on to his possessions. While George complained about being stuck, he unfortunately spent more energy complaining than getting off dead center. To him, giving up any of his luxuries for a new lifestyle would have been a step down.

During the 1985–86 slowdown in the Texas economy, I heard people complaining about having to take a major step backward. One acquaintance told how she and her husband had to sell their Mercedes and get a Buick. Another told of having to give up an exclusive membership to a local country club. The tone of the conversation held the same despair that I heard from Darrell when he lost his job. He and his wife and two kids had to move out of their three-bedroom house into a one-bedroom apartment.

Darrell, whose need for shelter had dropped him down to the first level of Maslow's need hierarchy, would have gladly traded woes with the lady who complained about having to sell her Mercedes. The Mercedes falls into the third and fourth levels of Maslow's hierarchy because it satisfies the need for belonging and self-esteem. Despite the differences between the need for shelter and the need for self-esteem, both Darrell and the Mercedes owner were threatened by their losses.

If a lifestyle change would require you to take a financial step backward, how far back would you be willing to go? Give up your mink? Give up your Cadillac? Give up eating out? Give up your car and use the bus?

How would you feel about giving up some things if, at the same time, you had less stress, more time with your family, felt better physically and had more time to do some of those things you have talked about doing before you die? I don't want to imply that a lifestyle change requires taking a financial step backward—but it may.

I have dealt with that question four distinct times in the past 25 years. The first time was after my first year as a math and science teacher in Denver. As young 21- and 23-year-olds, my wife and I had numerous discussions about world peace. It seemed that one way to help bring it about would be to get to know people from other countries at the grass-roots level. "To put our money where our mouth was," we volunteered to teach in Malawi, Central Africa. Those three years were a step backward in terms of material wealth, but they were a terrific step forward in other areas of our lives.

Our second financial step backward occurred when I decided to go to graduate school at age 29. Our two sons were four and seven, so the decision was somewhat more compli- cated. We had to decide whether I should keep my job and go to school part-time so we could remain living where we were, or give up my job and go to school full time. I decided to go to school full time. To make ends meet, we moved from our two-bedroom rented house and became house parents of a coed dormitory. Talk about adding stress to your life!

The third financial setback occurred when I was "let go." I had to decide whether to accept a job offer or go into business for myself. Going into business for myself was risky and initially would be a definite financial step backward. I had to decide what I was willing to give up. A lot of time was spent weighing the pros and cons. I decided to give it a try and if we had to sell our house and rent a small place, that was acceptable as part of the risk. The most we would be willing to give up before I would get a regular job would be to move in with my parents in another state. Fortunately, we didn't have to go to those extremes, but we were emotionally prepared for a significant financial reversal in order to give self-employment a try.

Fifteen years later I sold my company, and my wife and I talked about what we wanted to do now. The boys were out of the house—one in graduate school, the other a sophomore in college. Karen wanted to spend more time on her art and music, and I wanted to slow down and finish writing a book that I had been working on for two years.

To have the money needed for these activities, we sold our four-bedroom house with pool, all our furniture and most of the other things we had collected during 25 years of marriage. We moved to our condo in Breckenridge, Colorado.

When we were getting ready to make our move, I went up and cleaned out the attic. Its contents filled a big two-car garage. There were things we thought we someday might want, or they were kids' keepsakes. The thought of having to buy or rent a big house just to store our things seemed a little absurd, but what should we get rid of? It all seemed so precious.

Too often when people get ready to move, they think about moving everything they own. When you move everything you own, you don't have to decide what to sell. But think of all that packing!

"I found it tough to think of letting go of all the furniture that we had carefully saved for," admitted my wife, Karen.

"Since I am an interior designer, clients would come to our house, and I felt it was important that the furniture we had was of good quality. I looked around the room and there was our five-year-old wood and glass dining room table which I finally convinced Ted that we needed—after 20 years of marriage. It was always difficult for Ted to realize how much good furniture cost.

"Every piece in the room had been picked for a reason, and now the thought of letting it all go was an adjustment. However, it wasn't as big an adjustment now as it would have been a year earlier. During the past 12 months I had been thinking more about what I wanted to do with my painting and music, so the importance of the furniture and other trappings was beginning to fade. One thing that I really did hate to sell was the baby grand piano we had for 15 years. I had given hundreds of piano lessons on it back when Ted was getting started in business.

"When I walked out in the garage and saw it full with the things from our attic, it made me realize how much stuff you can collect after being in a place for 17 years. The garage was full without bringing out any of the items from inside the house. It was tough to think about giving all that up—but it was our choice.

"We ended up having to rent a 10 x10 storage area for some of the things we couldn't sell right away, plus some of the keepsakes. The things we put in storage we felt had more sentiment—some of our history related to our two boys. And while I thought how important those things were at the time we stored them, right now I couldn't tell you what is in storage.

"If people are going to make a lifestyle change, I feel it is important to be willing to get rid of the things that might hold them back. Lots of things can be like a lead weight around your neck, which makes it difficult to move."

I was pleased that Karen was open to selling the things we did. I had a number of husbands say to me, "How did you ever get your wife to agree to sell all your furniture and other stuff?" Actually, it was probably harder for me to let go of things than for Karen because I am the pack rat in our family. I always hated to think of selling something one day and needing it the next.

What would you be willing to get rid of to make a lifestyle change? To live a life with less stress and more time to smell the roses? To help find an answer, take a paper and pencil and walk around your house, touching all the different pieces of furniture and other items that, if you got down to basics, you really wouldn't need. If you got rid of them how would you feel? Could you use the money from selling them to help grease your slide for change?

"I would have answered that question differently a year ago than I would today," was the response from Billie, who used to cling to every piece of furniture she owned. "Six months ago our house burned down and all that stuff that I thought was so terribly important is gone. I now realize how much value I was putting on material things when really what is important is life. I am so thankful I got out of the fire safely. My advice to other 'clingers of stuff' like I was, is to forget about stuff and go for life."

If you have the financial resources, you may be able to make a lifestyle change without having to give up anything. If that is the case and if you still feel stuck, what is keeping you stuck? Is it friends, your position in the community, children, parents, exactly what is it? There are always some tradeoffs that need to be weighed. Just remember, you are not getting any younger.

STUCK—WITH OR WITHOUT MONEY

One young lady asked, "How do you make a move in your life when you don't have cash reserves to fall back on? If you don't have a house to sell?" If you want to do it badly enough you will find a way. Move in with several other roommates instead of having your own apartment. Buy your clothes from the Salvation Army or other places that sell second-hand clothing. Give up eating out. Cut out going to the movies. You may not be doing all the things you used to spend a lot of money on, but if you are enjoying a richer life, you won't miss them.

It's when we are bored that we turn to outside things to add excitement to our lives. It is all in the perception. The bottom line is life—life with an emphasis on quality not quantity.

To be able to make ends meet may take some real discipline—depending on what financial resources you have in reserve. Are you disciplined about spending or are you one of those people we read about in the newspaper who has become carried away with all the credit cards available today? You need to ask yourself why you are relying on credit. Have you just decided to follow in the footsteps of Uncle Sam and say you are going to cut back spending, but just talk about it and never do it? Just saying you're going to cut back doesn't do the trick. It takes discipline combined with a strong sense of purpose for your life.

When 27-year-old Nancy was asked why she relied so heavily on credit cards, her answer was,"I would like to cut back, but it is hard. I want what my friends have. I want to look beautiful, have nice clothes, have pretty jewelry and I can't afford what I want on my salary. Now I have gotten myself in a trap. All my single friends think I have more money than I really do. I've got to maintain that image, to be able to go to the clubs, outings, etc. Maybe I'll luck out and marry a sugar daddy and he will pay my cards off for me."

Jack Wells, a CPA who made a lifestyle change at age 42, commented on discipline. "I look at young people and they are buying everything known to man. My biggest advice is not to buy all that stuff and don't buy on time. I never had a credit card until I was 46 years old. I left the company I had been working for after 17 years. I had a lot of my colleagues come up and say, 'I wish I could afford to quit.' As the controller of the company, I knew how much they were making. In most cases they were making as much or more than I was. I remember helping those guys with their personal income tax and I was constantly amazed at how little they saved—they threw it away somehow or the other. The difference was that my wife and I never spent all the salary we were making. If we hadn't been careful about our spending, I suppose we would still be stuck back there at the company just dreaming about what we are now doing."

As you look at your quality of life, are you depressed because you feel stuck over the lack of money? At the same time, are you currently making more money than you ever dreamed you would make? Did you ever think that anyone making as much money as you are making would ever have financial problems? I didn't! Admittedly, inflation has played some part in the adjustment of our thinking, but a bigger factor is often that our standard of living grows as fast or faster than our salary.

Can you imagine making over $100,000 a year and being stuck in a job that you can't afford to leave because of monthly financial commitments? That is exactly what has happened to Bill, a 47-year-old attorney:

"I would like to quit my law practice and do something else, but I can't because I have to keep making good money in order to meet my monthly commitments. Things have gotten out of hand, but I plan to turn that around before it gets any worse. When I was in law school, I had an old Ford that was as dependable as you would find them. After getting out of school, I was embarrassed to go to the country club in my old car so I bought a Buick. Then that wasn't good enough and now I have a Mercedes 450 SL.

"When the two girls came along, my wife was always concerned over how properly dressed they were. Then it was sending them to private schools where our friends were sending their kids.

"Now I am 47 years old and deeper in debt than ever. My wife and I have discussed scaling down our lifestyle. While on one hand she agrees that we need to cut back, on the other hand she feels that 'you only go around once,' so enjoy it now. I think we could have just as much enjoyment without having to spend quite as much. I am prepared to give up my Mercedes so I don't have to work so hard to make ends meet."

When you make the amount of money that Bill makes, there is a real temptation to buy things that really aren't needed—you just think you need them. There is always another good deal that will save you money if you buy it now and don't wait until tomorrow. How many things do you have sitting around your place that you bought because they were a good bargain?

After getting her divorce, Mary Lee had to go back to work. Working full time brought an unexpected benefit. "I don't have time to go through all the ads in the newspaper and see all those things that make me want to buy them. I am much happier now without this temptation. I don't have time to walk through the stores and see all the clothes I really don't need and probably would have ended up buying before. I avoid temptations that make me want material things—material things that just clutter my life."

The good news about stepping back financially is that as you start focusing on what is really important in your life, adjusting to having fewer material possessions won't be as difficult as you think right now. However, if you currently feel like less of a person if you don't have all the physical trappings, it is going to take a significant effort to shift from building your self-image with things to building it with a true belief in yourself. What you own is not important, but rather what you are as a person, as a creation of God.

Family counselor Dixie Agnew has found, "If you make the plunge and make a big lifestyle change, there are no guarantees in life that you are going to make a lot of money and that you are going to conquer the world. If your whole self-concept is tied up with the amount in your bank account, then change may be an emotionally chancy thing. It's important to take a careful look at how much of your self-image is tied up in your material possessions.

"It is not easy to make a value change. That is something that has to be thought through for a long time. Values are very basic to the way we think. Some have found that what they thought was a value really wasn't. You may find that other things in life are really more important than what you now are holding onto as being important. Other things may matter more than you realize."

*Creeping Tastes (Or, The Spirit Was Willing
But the Flesh Was Weak)*

For the three years Karen and I were teachers in Africa, we were on a voluntary service basis, which provided a small allowance to cover room, board, clothing, plus $15 per month—just enough to buy film, stamps and a few African curios. Needless to say, materialism wasn't an issue for us. In fact, it was repulsive to hear some of the American Embassy personnel complaining about their "tougher living standards" because the house they were living in did not have parquet wood floors. We were pleased just to have shiny black cement floors.

While most people wondered how we handled the culture shock of arriving in Africa, we found it was a bigger shock to come back to the States. When we got back, we immediately noticed how much time was spent talking about things, or about activities at the country club. We decided one thing for certain—we didn't want to fall into that materialistic trap. Well, the spirit was willing but the flesh was weak. Tracing our progression from 1965 to 1985 looks like this:

1965—Bought all the furniture for our two-bedroom 800-square-foot rental house—for $500 (including washer and dryer); Bought all clothes for ourselves and our two-year-old son from Penney's and Sears; Drove a square-back Volkswagon.

1967—Bought clothes from more expensive stores; Have five suits instead of just one.

1969—Bought 2,000-square-foot house with a large stone fireplace and a two-car garage.

1970—Became good friends with a bank president and his wife—went to a lot of nice clubs where he was a member; Felt pressure to buy name-brand clothes and better-quality shoes. Were getting embarrassed by our square-back Volkswagon, so we bought a two-year-old Grand Prix.

1971—Lost my job and watched every penny.

1973—Bought clothes at name-brand stores once again.

1974—Bought a used Toyota for second car.

1975—Bought a two-year-old Continental Mark IV.

1976—Bought 3,200-square-foot house and put in a large swimming pool.

1977—Spent $2,000 for a sofa.

1978—Went to Germany, Alaska and Hawaii (with two kids); Bought a new Mercedes; Went on Caribbean cruise.

1979—Bought a new Buick Skylark for second car.

1980—Bought two rental houses in Dallas.

1981—Bought one-and-a-half condos in Breckenridge—payments $2,000 per month.

1984—spent $4,000 for minor remodeling in master bedroom.

1986—Sold business; Sold house and all furniture; Put rental houses up for sale; Moved into 1,200-square-foot condo in Breckenridge.

I share this history because it shows how easy it was for us to get caught. People standing on the sidelines might have said we were trying to keep up with the Joneses. I never felt that was the case, but maybe it was. At the time I would have stood on a soapbox and proclaimed that I wasn't caught up in materialism. But maybe I could have turned down some out-of-town speaking engagements and gone to a few more of my sons' basketball games and track meets.

The rental houses and condos were bought as investments. Unfortunately, the interest rates for the condos went up to 16 percent before we closed the deal. When my business had a slowdown, the crunch was felt. From this experience I can clearly see how people can get themselves into a financial rut that becomes a grave.

When discussing materialism, it is important to differentiate between business and personal purchases. Farmers, for example, put everything back into their farms. Quite often you will find a very modest farmhouse and a big tractor out in the field—a tractor that might cost over $100,000. My uncle Nelson, a Kansas farmer, reminded me of the saying that farmers live poor and die rich because they put everything back into the farm.

As you look at your life, in what way have your tastes slowly gotten more expensive? How would your life be different today if you had clung to a more basic lifestyle? Are you experiencing stress right now because you have overextended yourself with all your credit purchases? Is that putting you in a rut that is becoming a grave? Is your life on hold because of Jones-phobia?

SUMMARY: THOUGHTS ON JONES-PHOBIA

Jones-phobia affects everyone's life in our commercialized affluent society. It's a commitment to having more, and moving ahead, with the motivation that more is better. Worrying about not keeping up can prevent us from focusing on the quality of life we desire.

Why is the Jones-phobia so destructive? Let's listen to the words of a 57-year-old man, Alexander, who lay in his bed dying of cancer. "I am going to die and all the things I have collected during my life have little value now. I worked hours and hours trying to have a nice home for my family. We could have gotten along with a lot less. I didn't have much time for community activities and church work. All I am leaving behind now is some wealth for my kids to fight over. I wish someone had taken me by the ear and helped me get my priorities straight before now. My main concern was the next business deal around the corner."

Is your life directed toward greater fulfillment? Or are you headed down the dead-end road of materialism?

Do you own your possessions or do they own you? As I hear people talk, I get the impression that the possessions own them. They tell how hard they have to work to make payments, how they don't have time to eat lunch, how they have to work weekends and can't spend time with their families. You don't hear the possessions complaining.

After making lifestyle changes, people have found they have a fresh new perspective on the ruling power of money and materialism. Only after stepping back and looking over their total life could they see how money had monopolized a lot of their thinking. Is this also true of your life?

Interestingly enough, those who had lots of money at one time really weren't all that concerned about having it again. Certainly they weren't going to break a gut to get it. It was as if their curiosity had been satisfied and now they were going to focus on the quality of life rather than the quantity.

"I love my THINGS—my collections of bells, plates and curios and commemorative stamps—because of the precious memories they evoke," wrote my 92-year-old friend, Bernice Anderson. "Nothing was chosen to impress anyone; they were chosen either because of what good times or places they recall, or for the memories certain inherited pieces bring to mind. I even like some pieces of furniture and/or decor, not for their money-value, but because I revel in the beauty of color and design. I love making floral arrangements and just sitting or lying back and enjoying the warmth of their colors. I feel that things of this kind are like familiar companions when one grows too old to be as active as one would like to be. They are almost as precious as are my many friends. Many of my beloved friends and relatives have departed from this world, but I still have mementos reminding me of them!"

In the 24 years I have known Bernice, I have never seen her life on hold. While she has collected a lot of things, her life is dedicated to people, not things.

Most of the people I interviewed felt the majority of their friends and acquaintances would not make a lifestyle change because they would hate to take the chance of giving up their comfortable style of living. But they also thought that if these people decided to make a change, they would probably be surprised how their new priorities would affect their lives.

While it is not always necessary to step back materially to make a lifestyle change, there needs to be a willingness to step back if necessary. Such an attitude gives more flexibility of movement. It's one thing for the average person to make a lifestyle change that requires $4,000 a month to live and quite something else if a person can get by on $900 a month. Some people who make lifestyle changes find they can't afford their new freedom when the bills keep piling up. They have to either cut back or go back to their old way of living—and a few go back.

The words *comfortable living* kept popping up in the interviews. It became apparent that what was a comfortable living to one might be a sacrifice to another and vice versa. One lady had to give up her live-in maid and do her own cleaning. Another fellow gave up his Jaguar for a beat-up Toyota. For some, a sacrifice was not being able to eat at a nice, dress-up restaurant at least once a week. For others, eating at McDonalds once a week was a luxury. What does "a comfortable living" mean to you?

There did not appear to be any relation between the amount of money spent and quality of life. I remember the excitement Karen and I felt when we got a brand-new washer and dryer after 10 years of marriage. That excitement was as great as when we later got our new Mercedes. In a recent TV interview, Ross Perot also told how he was just as excited about the things he and his wife had early in their marriage as he now is with his millions.

When comparing quality of life with the quantity of life, it is easier to measure quantity for we can put a dollar amount on it, while quality is an intangible feeling of well-being. While these two measures are in different camps, we often confuse them with each other—adding a lot of confusion to our lives.

Some people are more confident in their life decisions than others. They have more belief in their ability to conquer whatever problems and challenges might arise. The greater self-confidence people have, the less they worry about keeping up with the Joneses.

Sarah, a store clerk, found a definite tie between her self-confidence and need to buy, buy, buy. "I used to worry about what others thought of me and it seemed that I was always comparing myself with others. If someone at work had a new dress, it made me feel that I was a slouch unless I got something as nice. I couldn't keep up that buying pace—my cards were charged to the limits. It was then that I started working on my personal confidence of who I was. Little by little I got to feeling more confident about me as a person regardless of what I wore or drove. That helped cut down my need to spend."

How do you see your spending habits relating to your self-confidence? Do you find that there are some days you feel less confident than others and have an urge to go shopping?

When people really start looking at how they can handle the finances of a lifestyle change, options will start surfacing that they had never thought of before. Writing ideas down as they come to mind helps get the ball rolling. In some cases it takes several years to get a clear picture of how to progress. If you really want something, there is usually a way to make it work if you are willing to be flexible and patient.

If you feel trapped and decide to make a major shift in values, you will need another significant priority to replace the old value, otherwise you are just left with a vacuum. The earlier chapters of this book discussed how to decide what you really want and how to set new priorities that will add richness to your life.

As I walk outside and look at the beautiful mountain scenery, I ask myself, how would I ever convert this to dollars? Is this worth more than an evening out on the town? Is it worth more than $1,000? It's free for the looking. The perceived value depends upon a person's appreciation of this type of beauty. If someone's value system is concerned mainly with things that have a dollar sign, then this beauty is only worth a passing glance.

A recent TV newscast announced, "America's real pastime is making money,"—followed closely by shopping. Jones-phobia at work.

OVERCOMING JONES-PHOBIA

If you would like to overcome Jones-phobia and TAKE YOUR LIFE OFF HOLD, carefully go through the activities and questions that follow.

1. Looking at where and how you spend your time, is the accumulation of money and material possessions one of your main priorities in life?

2. Who do you most often try to impress with what you have? How would your life be different if they told you they really don't care about the things you have, that they are more interested in you as a person? Would you believe them? What would you do if you heard through the grapevine that if you didn't have that nice car and those club memberships, some of your friends would drop you?

3. If you were asked to give a talk to high school students on what you learned from material setbacks, what would you tell them?

4. In what way would you say (or someone else say), that your behavior suggests you are more interested in things than people? More interested in people than things?

5. What percentage of your time do you spend working and thinking in each of these areas:

percentage of time working		percentage of time thinking
	SELF-ACTUALIZATION	
	SELF-ESTEEM	
	BELONGING AND LOVING	
	SECURITY	
	FOOD AND SHELTER	
100 %		100 %

6. Walk around your home and make a list of things you would be willing to give up if it meant a better quality of life.

7. Everything you accumulate has its price. Its price can be measured in the amount of hours you work to get it or how much time it took away from your family and friends, or how it affected your health. Take some time to think about what you give up to accumulate material wealth. Things can be replaced; it's harder to replace family and friends.

8. Take at least five minutes daily for a week to write down how you are caught up in Jones-phobia. Do this exercise even if you don't think you are caught up in it. Living in our society makes it impossible not to be caught up in some way.

9. How would it affect your self-image if you were making one-half as much money as you are now making? How would it be affected if you were making twice as much?

10. For your own self-development, start paying close attention to how people associate their self-worth with material worth. What did you learn about yourself by watching them?

11. To have the flexibility required to make a change, it is necessary to carefully manage your money. Make a list of how you have wasted money in the past, how you waste money now and how you want to start managing your money. What could you do to increase the amount you save by 15 to 25 percent a month?

12. What would you be willing to give up to make a lifestyle change if it meant a better-quality life for you?

GREASING THE SLIDE FOR CHANGE

Change is scary. It is interlaced with uncertainties that cause some people to stay where they are. Others venture forward leaving a map to help those who choose to follow. Every life-style change is different; every person is different. Yet there is a bond of common experiences. These experiences help grease the slide for those waiting on the sidelines to make a break.

Insights gained from each chapter of this book are part of the preparation you can use to help alleviate fear and uncertainty. These insights become the tools that you use to help clear the path to change—the path to a more fulfilling life.

Nature, in its own innocent way, has lessons to stimulate our imaginations. Several times a week I hike up to a nearby mountain lake. The awesome beauty and sacred quietness opens my thinking to new ways of looking at life.

While I was working on this chapter, the ice on the lake was beginning to break up. From one end of the lake, the melting water emptied into a little mountain stream. Chunks of broken ice were floating along, some getting stuck between boulders jutting out in the stream.

The flowing water and chunks of ice reminded me of people. Some go with the flow and others get stuck between the boulders. Which are you? What are the boulders that are holding you back?

Is your thinking frozen? Do obstacles keep you stuck? Do you have an image you are trying to protect that keeps you from flowing with new ideas? Rigidity in your thinking can keep you from arriving at the destination you dream of.

To grease your slide for change, you need insight into your-self and an understanding of the obstacles in your way. Once you understand these obstacles, you can maneuver around them as you chart your course.

Which is easier? Removing the boulders or being more flexible yourself? Removing boulders will help speed your path downstream, but farther along you may run into other obstacles that require even greater skill and flexibility to maneuver around.

Are you afraid to go with the flow? Are you afraid where the stream might take you? You have the choice of staying stuck or going for what you want. The more flexible you are, the easier it will be for you to go with the flow and to enjoy the trip as well as the destination.

GREASING THE SLIDE WITH FLEXIBILITY

How would your life be different if you were more flexible and were able to go with the flow? Your flexibility is a key ingredient in making a lifestyle change. The more flexible you are, the easier it will be.

A flexible mind is like a flexible body. I remember a young man who fell 25 feet off our barn roof. Because his body was so limber when he hit the ground, he wasn't hurt. If he had stiffened up, he probably would have broken some bones. (I have yet to figure out how you can fall and be relaxed, but he did.) Likewise, the more flexible your thinking, the fewer broken brain cells.

The more flexible you are, the easier it is to weave through obstacles without getting bruised. People who are rigid in their thinking aren't able to adapt as well. When something unexpected comes up, they fall apart. In making any sort of change, you need to expect the unexpected. Exercise your flexibility by starting to do little things differently in your life.

Connie Westbrook, a loan officer, exercises her flexibility by "getting in groups or connecting with people who motivate me to see things in new ways. These women are more likely to reach out and help knock me out of old patterns that aren't fulfilling. I look at ways to knock me out of my comfort zone even if I create my own crisis. It forces me to face new things and grow in new ways. It is easy to get rigid in our thinking and just gripe about things.

"One way I see to begin getting out of a rut is to throw yourself into completely new situations. Even such simple things as changing where you do your grocery shopping, the route you drive to work, the time you get up, when you go to bed, where you sit at the dinner table, where you sit in church. When I make these kinds of changes, I then evaluate what I miss about the old and what new I have learned in making the change. Our comfort zones may feel comfortable but they may also unknowingly be doing us a disservice in holding us from experiencing the new."

What have you done recently that demonstrates your flexibility? Would you describe yourself as being flexible and able to adapt to new situations, or does the unexpected drive you crazy? What are you doing to help increase your flexibility?

Being a person who likes to be in control, when things seem to be in disarray I have to step back and take a deep breath. It helps me to remember that while the moment may seem terribly critical, it isn't a matter of life or death. This helps you go with the flow—which helps grease the slide for change.

GREASING THE SLIDE TO SAY GOOD-BYE

Saying good-bye to friends and family is tough. What will you miss most about them when you move? Is it the fun you have with them? Is it being able to share your thoughts with those who know and understand you? Or do you fear that when you move you won't be able to make any new friends?

"Some people find change as stressful as a divorce or a death," said minister Allen Nesbitt. "There is the difficult experience of losing associations. Even though you weren't comfortable with them the way they were, you can trust them in a certain sense. There is a new geographic setting. There is the separation from current friends, moving into neighborhoods where you are not known. The familiar is gone."

What does Allen suggest for greasing the slide for change? "Being a churchman, one of my suggestions in dealing with change is to see the church as your family—like you are going home. One thing I have learned from military officers who move around a lot, as soon as they get into a new community, they get involved in the church and it becomes instant family." Karen and I also have found this helpful when making a transition. The first Sunday we were in Breckenridge, we went to a local church. It helped us feel at home right away. We have always been active in the church and have found it helps us settle into a new community.

Some of the people I interviewed told how slow it was to make friends, while others in the same community said how easy it was. The difference of opinion often reflected how involved these individuals were in church and community activities.

When you visit places, get to know the town folks. Jim Stanley, 48, an attorney, and his wife, Sue, vacationed in the same place year after year. "Each time we went back we went to church, and little by little we began to know some of those folks. When we got ready to make a lifestyle change, it made it easier knowing the area and also knowing some of the people at the church."

As might be expected, some of those left behind have a stronger feeling of loss than the person making the change. When you make a lifestyle change you will be filled with emotions, including excitement about the new adventure, while those left behind remain in their familiar setting.

Some people remain stuck in a lifestyle because their friends and family don't want to lose them. Other people, like Nancy Stider, 28, go ahead and make a move because they feel they can carry the love of their friends with them.

Nancy had to think a long time before leaving her California friends. "I wanted to see some of the rest of the country before getting married, so I gave up my good job and moved to a resort area to work. All my friends were hitting their jobs hard and here I was thinking about quitting and making a change. We had taken vacations together, cried together, laughed together.

"While I really miss my friends, I have been able to keep my good friends even though we live a thousand miles apart.

Thank heavens for the telephone. When they come out to see me, we are able to pick up where we left off. We are still very close."

The women I interviewed tended to miss their friends and family more than the men did. Although there are exceptions, one possible generalization is that men often do not get as attached in friendships as women do.

Early childhood experiences can affect our relationships today, as Jim Stanley found. "I grew up in a situation where we moved around a lot, and I instinctively did not form close friendships. There are a lot of people I appreciate and respect, but as far as growing up in a situation where I had a friend I couldn't do without, I never did."

Which of your experiences influence how you pursue friendships today? Do you feel it is easier for other people to say good-bye to their friends than it is for you? Why?

While it is hard to leave the comfort of seasoned friend-ships, a new lifestyle opens the door to the excitement of mak-ing new friends. Every change Karen and I have made has put us in contact with interesting people, some of whom have be-come close friends.

Rather than focusing your attention on the friends you are leaving, grease your slide for change by focusing on the stimu-lation of the new friends you will meet.

Although the people I interviewed said they hated to leave their friends, it was not a major issue to them. In some cases, they seemed glad to get a little space from some of their rela-tionships. As Andrea, 42, a bank teller put it, "We liked our friends, but it was getting to the point that if we did anything we had to ask this other couple along. Sometimes we wanted to reach out and meet new people and these other friends would get upset about our not wanting to spend more time with them."

Have you ever needed a little space from some of your friends? How did you go about getting it? A lifestyle change can help. As you change your life, many of your friends will also change, regardless of whether or not you make a geographic change.

GREASING THE SLIDE BY KNOWING
THE GEOGRAPHIC AREA

When lifestyle changes included a geographic move, most of those interviewed had previously visited the new area several times on vacations. With each visit they found it harder to go back home, until finally they decided to make a lifestyle change combined with a move.

"We came out here every year and stayed as long as we could," Jack Wells said. "Jean and I dreaded going back to work again. Each time we left we would be thinking, 'Oh, we have to wait until next year to do this again.' Finally the third year we said, 'Why are we doing this? Why don't we stay out here and do something?' We decided to try it and see what happens and if we don't like it we can sell it and do something different." After 17 years as a CPA with the Mayo Clinic, Jack and his wife, Jean, opened a bed-and-breakfast lodge—and they love it.

Have you ever visited a place and said to yourself I wish I could live here? Do you find yourself going back there time and time again? Is it harder to leave each time? How would your life be different if you lived there?

Perhaps you don't have a special place. All you know is that you would like to move from where you are. Start exploring other areas where you might like to live. Next time your friends come back from a vacation and they tell you how wonderful it was, ask them lots of questions about the place. It might be somewhere you would like to explore. Or you may decide it is definitely not for you. If you loved the night life and thought the shopping was terrific, you might want to visit there if you like night life, but it might be a real turnoff if you are more interested in the outdoors. What is great for one person may be terrible for another.

A lot of people who have moved to their favorite vacation spot, never dreamed they would be living there. It was going back time and time again that started the wheels turning.

GREASING THE SLIDE BY GETTING FINANCES IN ORDER

For most people, being able to afford a lifestyle change is a major concern. While they would like to make a change, they don't think they have enough money set aside.

How much money is enough? During a casual party conversation, one man said, "I would love to make a lifestyle change but until I have a couple hundred thousand set aside for the kids' college, I need to stay where I am."

Another man responded, "Surely you can get by for less than $200,000 for two kids. Let them go to a good state school."

This conversation illustrates how everyone needs different amounts before they will feel comfortable in making a change.

Sometimes lack of money is an excuse for not making a change. The real reasons are submerged. You might really be stuck by a lack of direction, or a strong fear of the unknown, or not wanting to give up a high-stepping lifestyle.

How much money do you want to have saved before making a lifestyle change? "When I first thought about making a lifestyle change, it was financially impossible for me to leave my position at IBM," was Betty Schuldt's response. "My debt level was so high I couldn't afford to take a pay cut. So I put the thought on hold until I lowered my debt level. Then I had a wonderful turn in sales that gave me some big commission checks for a couple of months and I was able to reduce it. If I hadn't taken care of some of those bills before I moved, I would have had people climbing all over me."

When Betty moved she took a 50-percent pay cut, but her quality of life took a significant jump. She now is able to combine her work with some of the leisure activities she really enjoys. But before being able to make the change, she had to get her finances under control.

Are your finances out of control? What are you doing to get them in shape so you can make a lifestyle change? Are you willing to give up a little now so you can have more later?

It's the little amounts that add up. It amazes me when I buy groceries. Those little 50-cent items add up to a total that always makes me think the clerks misfigured. But they didn't.

The reverse is also true. If you save a little here and there, you will be surprised how fast it adds up. Monica Brown, an executive secretary, said, "I used to eat out a lot—normally at inexpensive places. For one month, I decided to only eat out once a week. Every time I had the urge to eat out, I would estimate how much I would have spent, then I estimated how much I was going to spend eating at home and the difference I put in a little glass jar. I called it my 'joy jar.' I even packed my lunches for work. That month I put over $180 in the joy jar. I couldn't believe it. That is over $2,000 a year. It made me wonder how much other money I am unknowingly wasting."

Have you ever kept track of how much money you spend for different things? Were you surprised? Most people spend all they make. It takes discipline and planning to save. Disciplining your spending habits makes it easier to make a lifestyle change.

How little do you think you could get by on in the following areas?

1. *Insurance—health, life, car.* If you get rid of your car and use public transportation or a moped or a bicycle, you will save money on car insurance, repairs, maintenance and gas. While it may seem extreme at first, some have found it to be the answer for getting their budget under control. Have you considered raising the deductible amount on your insurance policies? The larger the deductible, the smaller the annual premium.

2. *Food.* How much would you save if you didn't buy any junk food, ate more beans and less steak, more oatmeal and less packaged cereal? Talk to friends of yours who know how to stretch a grocery dollar. How do they do it?

3. *Clothes.* Look at your closet. How many name brands jump out at you? How much would you have saved if you hadn't bought name brands? Are there any good second-hand shops in your area? Are you willing to wait for sales instead of buying things when they first come out?

4. *Utilities.* Do you keep your place real cool in the summer and real hot in the winter? Are there some rooms that

don't need to be heated or cooled on a regular basis? When you leave for work, do you adjust the thermostat to help save costs?

5. *Charge Cards.* Charge cards are often an indication of how much you are financially out of control. If you owe $2,000 and you make $20,000 a year, you are 10 percent out of control. See if you can stop using them entirely. It's tough at first since you will be paying cash for everything you buy and also paying off what you owe on the cards. How much monthly interest are you paying on your charge cards?

6. *Entertainment.* Get creative and do simple things like old-fashioned picnics in the park, free church recitals or playing games with friends instead of going out. People are often surprised how a movie here and a drink there add up so fast. How much do you spend on things that you could do without?

7. *Rent.* Are you living in a place that costs you more because of the address or all the special extras like swimming pool and recreational facilities? Are you using those facilities? If so, great. How much could you save if you moved to something more modest?

8. *House Payment.* If you are paying a high rate of interest, explore refinancing your house. Some mortgage companies now have a payment plan where you pay every two weeks instead of once a month. This will save you considerable money over the term of a mortgage.

These are some of the major items that need your consideration as you prepare for a lifestyle change. This is not a comprehensive evaluation of your finances. Rather its purpose is to shed light on how to control your spending. As you start looking at each area of your life, you will be surprised how much fun you can have for less.

Your new budget will also give you a baseline for developing a budget for your lifestyle change. As you learn to live on less, you won't need to have as much set aside before making your lifestyle change. It will be an easier transition if you can painlessly survive on $1,000 a month rather than $2,500.

Since making our lifestyle change, Karen and I have cut back our monthly expenses by 75 percent. We have cut back from 18 tanks of gas every six weeks to just one. We seldom eat out. Our biggest expense has been a pair of season ski passes. At the same time our expenses went down, our quality of life went up.

When finances are of concern, greater creativity is needed to plan fun activities. Connie Westbrook has always been excited about life, even when she was penniless. "If you have a good feeling about yourself and if you can be excited about the free things in life—sunrises, flowers, everyday things like a warm bath—if you can act like a child and approach and enjoy it as a child, it gives you a good warm glow about yourself without having to buy things to make you feel good or rely on other people to make you feel good. It comes from inside, therefore no one can take it from you."

Are you creative about thinking of inexpensive fun things to do? Can you go on a vacation and have a great time without spending a lot of money? If you have limited funds and think you must spend money to have fun, it will be difficult for you to make a lifestyle change unless you take a fresh look at what is really important in your life. Unless you have unlimited funds, you must be prepared to adjust your spending habits.

If you are unhappy where you are and are looking for a better quality of life, you need to decide what you are willing to give up to make a change. You may not have to give up anything, but you need to be mentally prepared in case it is necessary.

PUTTING YOUR THOUGHTS ON PAPER

When you put your thoughts on paper it helps clarify your thinking. I have always been surprised at the number of people who try to make complex life decisions while keeping it all in their heads. That is like a juggler trying to keep all the balls in the air at once. When you write things down, you don't have to worry about forgetting some of your thoughts—and the grayer the hair, the more I find this helps.

"I think a lot of people are afraid to write down things on paper," said Susan Francis who made a lifestyle change by leaving her prestigious home and live-in maid in Dallas. "When you put your thoughts on paper, it is like you are committing to that feeling—from mind to pencil to paper. I find it really helps me to write things down so I can see everything in front of me and not just circling in my head."

Mary Jane Burgess also found this helpful when she and her husband decided to make a lifestyle change by going overseas for three years:

"Once in a while, everyone needs to sit down and go over priorities. I make a list of the things I have done in the past month that were priorities, and the things I have let slide. Then I compare the two lists. I often find some things that are disturbing. I see how much time I spend on things that aren't on my priority list. It helps me see where I am spinning my wheels.

"When we talk, I think a lot of times we don't remember what we say. When we write it down, it suddenly becomes concrete. The first thing I would recommend for anyone contemplating a lifestyle change—whether it is basic or a move from one place to another—start out by making a list. Make a list of things like 'I'm tired of this rat race,' 'This is what I would like to do,' 'I want to move from this position to that position.'

"Keep a journal—sometimes called diaries. Journals are wonderful for putting down your feelings and what you were thinking. I write things in my journal one week and the next week I can't believe I thought that last week. Sometimes it makes a lot of sense and other times it's like I am losing it.

"In my journal I also write down what I want to do and the things I have to do to get where I want to go. If you are making a move you can cry a lot, but God is not going to move your furniture. You can't just sit back in your prayer tree and say, 'Here I am.'

"If you have journaled along the way, when you go back and look at it, you can say, 'That's not what I really want,' or 'My goals have changed since then.' Or maybe your goal has changed just slightly so some of the directions don't fit now like they did then."

I agree with Mary Jane. Having journaled daily since 1965, and on and off before that, I find the process valuable in two ways. Some days I have concerns about something coming up. By writing down my feelings, it is like I am writing a story about someone else and unemotionally watching it unfold. The journal is now helping me carry the concern. Looking back later, I often see I was worrying about things that never happened. I wasn't seeing the whole picture. I also see what portion of my energy was directed toward my goals and how much was spent preoccupied with activities that sidetracked me from them.

Have you ever kept a journal? If so, what do you feel you gained from it? If not, what difference do you think it would make to you today if you had done three years of journaling? Would it help you see why and where your life is on hold?

SELF-HELP BOOKS GREASE THE SLIDE

Some people grease the slide for change by reading self-help books. It gives them new inspiration to help them move ahead. "One of the best things I ever did was to start reading self-help books," said businessman Frank Moran. "I started reading all those that were out. I took Dale Carnegie. I was the most negative person in the world. I felt I was the stupidest person in the world. I couldn't talk to two people because I was so self-conscious.

"My boss dared me to read a book. I said, 'I don't dare you,' and took the book. It was *I Dare You*, by William Danforth. It took two months to get through it. June 21, 1967, I finished the book. My life changed. A person has to have a positive mindset. I had all this knowledge but I couldn't bring it forward because of my negative thinking."

Like Mary Jane, Frank found value in writing things down. "Something else that has helped me is to write down things I am capable of doing. I would recommend that for anyone. It may take you six months or a year. That helps you start programming your brain. You don't sit down and say to yourself, 'This next 15 minutes I am going to figure out what I am going to do the rest of my life.' That's not it. It takes time. Some know what they want to do so they program their minds with that. Others may be uncertain, so the mind is programmed with an attitude of searching for options."

TAKE ACTION

Frank found that while reading books and writing things down helped, he couldn't stop there. He had to act.

"I was so busy trying to think of something to do, when I should have gotten out and done something—not just sat around.

"This may be a terrible thing to say, but, quite frankly, most people are lazy. They don't have the gumption to get off their rears and do something. They will read about other people doing things, but they won't put the effort out themselves. They can read all kinds of ideas on how to change, but they have to make the effort. No one else can do it for them. And now I am talking about myself.

"During this time I was trying to find myself, I spent a Saturday and Sunday watching football. Sunday night Mary Jo said, 'Frank, when are you going to come back and be part of the family?' She was really honked. I was using TV as a way to escape. I just sat there and let it entertain me. It takes work to get out and do something."

Have you ever found yourself glued to the TV when you knew you should be out doing something? You have a lot of potential but you have to do something to let it out. If you just sit there, another year will go by with your life still on hold. Taking that first step is crucial. As you take each step, the next step becomes clearer. Each step helps to grease the slide for change. What is keeping you from taking that first step? What are you afraid might happen if you did?

Making a lifestyle change is like climbing a mountain. You can sit and think about climbing the mountain. You can wonder what you will find when you start climbing. But the only way you will find out is by taking that first step, then the next and the next. With each step you can see further. Some of the mystery of what is ahead of you will be answered by taking those initial steps.

When you are getting ready to start climbing a mountain, it is helpful to talk with others who have already successfully done it. They can suggest paths to take for the best climb. In the same way, people who have made lifestyle changes can give you information that will help you grease the slide for your own change. Who are some people you might talk to who have made a change? What questions are you going to ask them? What fears do you have in talking to them? There is a lot to be gained from O.P.E.—Other People's Experiences.

HOBBIES CAN GREASE THE SLIDE FOR CHANGE

Wouldn't it be great if you could quit your job and live off your hobby? How would you look at your life differently if you knew that in a year or two, you could give up the job you now dread and start doing your own thing? It takes some creative thinking but it can be done, as John Feight demonstrated.

John always loved art but only could afford to do it as a hobby:

"I was what you would call a 'Sunday painter.' I had been painting out of frustration ever since getting my first job out of college.

"I had painted enough that I was able to give an art show in Paris. It was at this art show that I took a serious look at my life. I had been in the corporate business world for 10 years and now was in the advertising and marketing department of a company with $400 million in sales. I had eight people working for me. While it was a good job, I was starting to feel that I wasn't doing anything with my life and my art—especially my life.

"I came home from Paris and volunteered at a hospital. As I was working, it dawned on me that my art could help people in the hospital. I could then do something of value with my life instead of just painting to compete or to sell.

"I started painting one mural after another in hospitals and got involved to the point that in 1981 in a Paris hospital, I made up my mind to figure out a way to leave my job. I started planning. I personally believe that when people figure out what they want to do with the rest of their lives, they shouldn't just jump off the cliff and not know where they might land.

"I had something that meant a lot to me. It meant so much to me that I didn't want to fail, so I didn't quit my job and suddenly say, 'now I am going to paint full time.' I knew where I wanted to go and I just had to figure out how to get there—it came over a three-year period of time.

"Historically, artists have said, 'Heck with the system. I am going to go paint,' and they have starved and they haven't achieved what they wanted to achieve. I didn't have money so I had to work within the system and have the system make this dream happen. To do this, I set up a nonprofit organization called The Foundation For Hospital Art.

"I took inventory of what I had. With all I had, there was enough money to last me one year. I made up my mind, regardless of what bad thing happened, I wouldn't make a decision before the year was finished.

"Often I think of the book *Jonathan Livingston Seagull*. The book encourages you to take risks and even make mistakes so you can learn from them. A lot of people hold back and stay within the security they think they have— as it is.

"I also like the story Richard Bach told in his book *Illusions* about the fish that clung to the side of the river. They are talking to each other saying, 'Don't let go because those that have, disappear down the river never to be seen again.' So the fish keep hanging on. The ones that let go become what they are destined to be and they discover a new world. There are some beautiful things that are going to take place in our lives—but we have to let go to experience them.

"There are good things that happen that you can't even predict, but most people will be rational about what they think will happen and they use logic—logic that is based on yesterday's experiences. People are holding back and holding on to the side of the river—holding on to things they can see and touch. They are not reaching out for tomorrow.

"The feelings I have now are so different than I had when I was caught up in the corporate world. It's something that is hard to describe—you have to experience it to really get the feeling."

John has received national recognition for his contribution of brightening up hospitals with his murals. He is assisted in his projects by volunteers—including my wife, Karen.

What John did took careful planning and working within the system. He had a dream and did not give up on it. What would you do if you could do anything you wanted? Where would you like to be doing it? What is holding you back?

CREATIVE THINKING GREASES THE SLIDE

Maybe your dream is to do what you are doing, but to do it in a beautiful location or in a smaller town. Your concern may be that your particular skill is not needed in the new location. Such was Sandy Turns's predicament.

Sandy, a computer operator, wanted to move but didn't want to give up a great job in data processing. After exploring different options, she was able to work out an arrangement with her company to allow her to connect through a remote terminal. This was a plus for Sandy because she could then move to the little town of her dreams. It was a plus for her company since it opened up another office and another parking spot—of which there was a shortage.

While at first glance you may feel tied to an area because of your specific occupation, brainstorm some ideas about how you might be able to make a change. Too often people see how others do it but can't see how to do it themselves. You can begin greasing the slide for change by letting your creativity flow. Don't be discouraged if the solutions don't seem to come the first several times; it sometimes takes weeks.

SUMMARY: THOUGHTS ON GREASING THE SLIDE FOR CHANGE

Making a lifestyle change is much like snow skiing for the first time. You can go to the top of the mountain, get off the lift and pray you get down without hurting yourself or someone else.

Or you can take a lesson to learn how the skis work, how to stop, and how to shift your weight from one ski to the next. By understanding the basics of skiing before going to the top of the mountain, you have a greater probability of coming down without a serious problem. Are you one of those people who go to the top of the mountain and pray you will make it down safely? Or do you learn as much as possible before going up? People who think they don't need lessons are also the ones who will tell you horror stories about the dangers of skiing. Likewise, those who jump from one thing to another without thought or planning will tell you horror stories about the dangers of making changes.

When you make a lifestyle change, you will be facing uncertainties. The more systematically you approach your change, the less stressful it will be. Even at best, some things will happen that you never expected. This is true of everyday living—with or without making a big change. Are there any particular uncertainties that are scary to you? How are you going to grease the slide for change to help reduce those fears?

If you understand your feelings and know what you would like to gain, you have already begun to grease the slide for change. The next step is to actually do something.

How will you be able to handle the change financially? If you have savings, that will make it easier. If you have enough to live on for six months to a year, you have time to get settled in without panic. Some people have that much; others don't. How much money you have right now depends in part on how much you make at your job, but a bigger variable is how you handle your money. Some people who make $100,000 a year are less able to make a lifestyle change than those who make $24,000. Knowing how to stretch each dollar is important. How well can you stretch a dollar? Lifestyle changes tend to focus on quality of life, not quantity. When you cut the quantity back, managing your checkbook becomes more critical.

Mental flexibility makes change easier. Plan each step as thoroughly as possible, then relax and go with the flow. Trust yourself that whatever unexpected happens, you will be able to handle it. Are you good at going with the flow or is that an area you are working on?

If your lifestyle change includes a geographic move, it will be easier to decide where you would like to settle if you have traveled a lot. Travel opens up your mind to differences between one area and the next. Most lifestyle changers have previously visited the area they decide to make their new home. They know what they are looking for. What are you looking for in a new area? Talk to people who travel a lot. They can give you ideas.

An ideal situation is to do your favorite type of work in your favorite location. This is more possible than you may initially think. You can make it happen through creative exploration—keeping an open mind and being flexible in your thinking. Write your ideas down. Your thinking may change from day to day. The more you have written down, the easier it is for you to track your thought progression. Daily occurrences can affect your priorities. For example, if you have had an especially good time with your friends, they will be more important to you than they would be if you had had several disagreements with them.

Exciting possibilities in life are often submerged and lost in everyday confusion. The better you understand the factors that affect your decision making and the variables that affect change, the easier it will be for you to make a lifestyle change. Greasing your slide for change helps turn your dreams into reality. You have more control over results when you are looking for them. Through understanding, fears are diminished.

QUESTIONS AND ACTIVITIES TO GREASE YOUR SLIDE FOR CHANGE

The following can help you make your change easier. You may also want to review and compare your responses to other related activities in previous chapters.

1. List some of your fears about change. What can you do to help grease the slide for handling them?

2. Make a list of your major monthly expenses. What can you do to reduce this total by 10 percent? By 15 percent? Let your mind go wild and see how you could reduce the total by 25 percent.

3. How would your life be different if you reduced your expenses by 25 percent as suggested above? Would that require a major sacrifice or just better control of your spending?

4. If you are going to make a geographic change, what five factors will influence where you are going to move?

5. List at least eight ways you would describe your thinking as being rigid. List five ways others might describe you as rigid.

6. Briefly describe five situations that illustrate your ability to go with the flow. What words do you think your friends would use to describe your flexibility?

7. Draw a picture of a stream with boulders jutting out that might stop you—a piece of ice—from being able to flow smoothly downstream. Draw as many boulders as you can think of related to your life. Below is a sample.

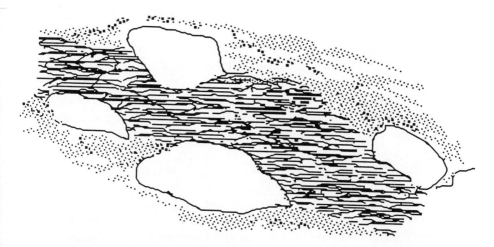

8. What would you need to change about yourself to move through the boulders? How could you get rid of the boulders?

9. How are you going to grease the slide for change when it comes to leaving your friends?

10. Write down three things you really enjoy doing. Creatively think of ways you could construct a lifestyle so you could do these things when and where you wanted.

11. Make a list of the things you are going to do to grease your slide for change.

FAMILY CONSIDERATIONS

WHEN COUPLES DON'T AGREE
ON MAKING A CHANGE

If you are wanting to make a change and your spouse doesn't want to, then you may have a problem on your hands. The good news is that it can be resolved, providing both of you are willing to work at it.

The couples I interviewed often remarked how fortunate they were because they saw eye to eye about making a change. The singles often remarked how they felt fortunate in not having to worry about anyone but themselves in their change.

But what happens if one spouse says, "I have to make a change or I am going to go crazy," and the other spouse responds, "If we make a change I will go crazy." If this is your dilemma, you might find a solution among those offered by the five professional counselors I spoke with.

David Stringer, a Presbyterian minister and counselor, said, "The place I would begin is with their value system and the sense of trust they have with the other's value system. I would help them explore that value system and see why that is important to them. I would ask, 'What is it you would like for her to hear and what is it you would like for him to hear? What is it about this place that is driving you crazy? Help your spouse understand that. What is the risk for you in terms of leaving?'

"Most times when people come to see me they are dealing with symptoms of the problem, but seldom the real problem. You hear about people getting divorced by how toothpaste is squeezed."

Dixie Agnew, a family counselor who left a growing urban practice to start over in a small mountain town, emphasized the importance of getting to the core of the issue, including finding out how committed the couple are to each other.

"If a couple came in to me with that problem, I would look to see if the husband and wife talked about the real issue. Marriage requires a lot of give and take and compromises all through life. It is important to not make an impulsive decision without checking it out with the partner. Are they planning this as a permanent change or is this just for a year or two? This is a good time for the couple to look at their life ahead of them and see how committed they are to the marriage. How many compromises are they willing to make for the sake of marriage? Is the relationship the primary thing in their life? There has to be some give and take.

"Sometimes one spouse feels bad if he/she is not as excited about the change as the other spouse. People respond differently to life situations. There also may be a difference in their comfort in risk taking. Maybe the husband is a big risk taker and the wife is a Missouri show-me type person who wants to see it before she commits herself. This can create constant conflict in their relationship."

Are you a "show-me" type or are you a risk taker? What kind of problems and tension has that caused you?

Allen Nesbitt, a Methodist minister and counselor who specializes in handling problem situations, agreed that tension arises when "one is ready to run the risk and the other is not:

"It is the cause of some divorces. It's tough. One of them wants to make a change. 'The kids are gone. Why do I have to keep working as hard as I am? Why are you working? Why are we both working? I am ready to make a change. Let's move to another part of the country. Let's do something for ourselves now. We have been doing all this stuff for the kids all these years; it is time to do something for us.'

"The other spouse says 'I am not ready. I like not having the kids here. Now we have more money to spend. We can now live the good life right here.'

"The only thing I am going to do is to ask a lot of questions and try to find out what kind of commitment they have to their marriage. If they have a strong commitment, I am going to ask them to talk about their careers and relationships. Talk about risk. See why one person is willing to take a risk and the other is not.

"If they have commitment to their marriage, I think they can work it out. They both may have to move toward the center. They can't both go off in their own direction unless you want to get into one of these new-fangled marriages where one does their thing on the beaches of San Diego and the other does their thing in the mountains of Colorado and once a month they get together in Las Vegas. I have never seen many of that kind of marriage work.

"Problems like this are not simple. They are different individuals and they have to hammer it out. It is work with a capital W. They have to be intentional about what is going on. They have to work at really hearing the other person. They each need to be asked if they have been totally honest in expressing their feelings in the past or have they held some things back?"

When you get upset, do you normally hold back your honest feelings or do you let them "all hang out"? How does your spouse react when you express your feelings?

"Some couples are like toddlers as they try to start expressing their true feelings," psychotherapist Ken Unruh's observed:

"It's a whole new experience—like learning to walk for the first time. I remember a couple in which the husband was the president of a large corporation and used to a lot of everyday pressures, but when it came to communicating in the marriage, he was starting out as a toddler—a toddler learning to communicate after 30 years of marriage.

"When two people are polarized in their thinking— one wants to do this and the other doesn't—often they are being reactive to each other rather than being factual. They need to get factual. This is accomplished by asking each of them to clarify and articulate what they want out of living. What do they want from each other? They take a look at their fears, doubts, dreams, wishes. They need to look at their basic needs and wants and how they are going to get them met. In looking at their life in this way, it is amazing how people find ways to agree and come to a common denominator.

"In this process it may be discovered that one partner is wanting to move because of a desire to run away from the current setting. The other partner may not want to make a move because of a basic fear of change. As these issues are dealt with, it gives a new frame of reference for discussion and sharing feelings. It is helping them get to the heart of the initial polarization."

From my own experiences in mediation work, I have also seen the importance of those in conflict getting to the heart of the issue. A lot of time can be wasted arguing when the real issues are hidden by a smoke screen. The parties themselves may not be aware that the core issue is being skirted. That is when there is significant value in having a professional counselor help unravel the differences.

At age 60, psychotherapist Bob Hendrix scaled down the size of his business to achieve a more comfortable lifestyle. How does he handle differences of opinions between his married clients? "I want to know what each of them will do and want to do. What kind of energy are they willing to put into solving this impasse? The differences in what they want to do have to be negotiated. That's just another area in the relationship that has to be worked out. When people already have a tendency to not get along, they will pick out different things to be the arena for debate. They will fight over finances, sex, lifestyle —it just becomes an arena to control the relationship. Sometimes impasses continue and, knowingly or unknowingly, the couples may have a lot invested to maintain that impasse."

Is there an impasse in your life that takes a lot of energy to maintain? If so, why do you hold on to it?

When I asked some of the couples how they would handle the situation if one wanted to make a change and the other didn't," Charles B— responded, "If you get to that point in your life and you were afraid to discuss the issue with your spouse, it is going to be very difficult to open up now. It should have been worked on all along. But in fact, if one wanted to do it and the other didn't, there is no substitute for just doing it and then whatever the consequences, work through it with a counselor. I don't think you can make a major lifestyle change in midlife without seeing a counselor to help make a smooth transition."

Mary Jane Burgess chuckled at the approach she and her husband take. "We solve differences of opinion by sitting down at the table and fighting. We get our feelings out in the open— or at least I do. I tend to get emotional a lot. It is a give-and-take. I say, 'This is where I want to go.' And he says, 'You must be out of your mind. I'm not going there.' Then the next week we might feel vice versa. We finally come to a common agreement and are happy about it."

How do you handle differences of opinion? Are you normally happy with the final outcome?

As couples look at change, it is valuable for each person to put down the forces they feel are pushing them toward change and away from change. Each does this on a separate worksheet; then the forces are compared. If the husband has some the wife doesn't have, he adds those to his diagram. The wife adds her husband's differing forces to her diagram. Now both the husband and wife's diagrams have the same forces.

George, 46, a construction manager, and Charlotte, 43, a secretary, did the following force analyses when considering a lifestyle change that would move them from Boston to a small resort community in Arkansas. Charlotte listed the following forces in her decision:

PUSHING FORCES			OPPOSING FORCES
looking for new surroundings	>	<	kids in school
feel stuck in a rut	>	<	will miss friends
friend has moved away	>	<	active in ladies' group
		<	will hate to leave aging parents
		<	loves house living in
		<	like bridge club

George's force analysis is as follows. Notice the different forces not mentioned on Charlotte's list.

PUSHING FORCES		OPPOSING FORCES
feel burned out in job	> <	has seniority in job
frustrated with rat race	> <	likes golfing buddy
feel finances out of control	> <	kids in school
want to try something new	> <	will miss friends
	<	enjoys home workshop

After combining Charlotte and George's lists, the force analysis looked like this.

PUSHING FORCES Geo./Char.				OPPOSING FORCES Geo./Char.		
7	10	looking for new surroundings	> <	active in ladies group	1	3
8	2	feel stuck	> <	aging parents	2	5
5	5	friends moved	> <	love house	5	9
8	0	feel burned out in job	> <	like bridge club	0	4
10	2	frustrated with rat race	> <	has seniority in job	8	0
5	2	finances out of control	> <	likes golfing buddy	7	0
5	5	want to try something new	> <	kids in school	3	10
			<	will miss friends	1	5
			<	enjoys home workshop	5	0
48	26	Total		Total	32	36

Independently, George and Charlotte assigned values to each force on the combined list. In cases where a spouse had no value associated with a force, such as George not being a part of Charlotte's bridge club, zero was written down.

As you can see, George had a higher total on the pushing side and Charlotte had a higher total on the opposing side. One of the big differences came from Charlotte's hating to move the kids and also hating to leave her beautiful home. She admitted that those two issues wouldn't be as important if the kids had some friends where they were going to move and if she had another nice house to move into. So George and Charlotte took the kids on a vacation to the town they were considering. While there, they met some nice people and the kids got to meet some new friends. One year later, after finding a nice house, they made their move.

Through the force diagrams, George and Charlotte could look objectively at each other's thinking. They analyzed the core issues involved, one issue at a time. This opened up communications and an acceptable solution was reached. If there hadn't been that openness George and Charlotte might have stayed stuck in a rut—or they might have gotten a divorce.

Do you have differences of opinion that you might like to break down into different forces to see if you can come to an agreement? Are you afraid to discuss the issues openly with the other person? If so, why?

As my dad said after 50 years of marriage, "Marriage is not a fifty-fifty deal. It is a hundred-hundred deal—both couples have to give 100 percent."

PARENTS' CONCERN FOR CHILDREN

Husbands and wives may be ready to make a lifestyle change but refrain from doing it because of their children. Or they may make it *because* of the kids. I found as many thinking one way as the other. Some parents are waiting until the children are reared to make a lifestyle change. This decision is based on the belief that making a move sooner would be detrimental.

Harold and Patsy would like to get out of the rat race and settle into a slower lifestyle. Although he could sell his company and have enough money to not have to worry, they feel it would be devastating to their three kids who are in junior high and high school. Harold remembered when he had to move as a fifth grader. "It was terrible. It was hard for me to make friends at the new school. I would never do that to my kids. When they are raised, then we are going to make a major change, but not till then."

Darla and her husband wanted to make a lifestyle change that involved a move. "My husband was really getting bored with his job and we were discussing making a move, but we waited until our kids were raised before we moved. We would have hated to pull up roots while the kids were still in high school. I would have never done that to them."

On the other side of the coin are parents who feel differently about making a move. "In my opinion, too many families think, 'What do the kids want?'" Martha observed. "If the kids say no, then we can't do it. We have never lived that way. If our kids would have said no to our change, we would have still come on."

Supporting Martha's feelings, Mary Jane Burgess said, "When our kids are raised there will be just my husband and me. They will go out and make their own lives. They leave you. I don't think we, as parents, can give our entire lives to our children, for when they leave, we have nothing left. We felt if we didn't make our change now, we would be too old to do volunteer work overseas."

What position would you take? Would you wait until the children were reared or would you make your lifestyle change now?

Some people standing on the sidelines will say parents are selfish if they make a decision to change when the kids don't want to. Others will see it as a great opportunity for the kids. Besides they will have their day to do what they want when they get older. How about a situation where the kids are basically on their own, and the parents sell the home place? Is that fair to the kids?

Karen and I struggled with this dilemma when we were thinking about our move. Even though both our boys were in college, we had lived in Irving for 17 years and in our current house for 11 years. The boys were used to coming home to a nice, big four-bedroom house with lots of room to spread out.

The boys also had a lot of themselves invested in the place. When we first moved into the house, the boys had spent one summer helping us remodel, followed by a summer helping me put in a pool and all the landscaping.

Because of my farm background, I believe that hard work is good for you at any age. I remember my sons complaining and complaining about having to work so hard when their friends were out playing. Now we were thinking about moving away, leaving it all behind.

We asked them how they would feel if we made a move. Both agreed that a 3,200-square-foot house and pool were a lot to take care of now that they were in college. Even with their consent, at times we get the impression that they don't feel they have a home anymore. They are used to a house, not a condo. And there are times when Karen and I have to remind ourselves that it isn't the structure that makes a home, it's the family feeling in the structure. Admittedly, when the boys do come home from college, there is not a lot of space to spread out, and that is an adjustment for all of us.

As you parents struggle with change and how it affects your children, realize that a move can be disruptive, but it can also provide some valuable lessons. We are hoping that our boys will be more flexible in making their own lifestyle changes since they have seen us do it.

Bob Heath, who gave up a million-dollar profit-sharing venture feels his lifestyle change will give his son more confidence. "I have overheard him telling his friends, 'You know what my dad did? We had this great house and he moved and he's doing something entirely different than he used to.' I gave my children a lot of confidence that things can be done."

Parents, what do you think your kids would say if you made a lifestyle change this year?

Parents with younger children tell of how their lifestyle change gave them more time for their families. Bill and Heather Jarski left Boston for a small town when the oldest boy was five. Heather explained, "We wanted to move someplace where people were considerate of each other. There we were, working, working, working. Bill was working 60 hours a week; I was home with the two little kids. There was no extra money even with all our working."

Bill added, "Andy grew from a baby to five years old. He had grown and I hadn't seen it. Now I am saying, 'Why aren't you growing?' He is growing, but because I am around him a lot more, I don't see him growing by leaps and bounds like I used to when I was putting in 60 hours a week at Sears. We work just as hard now, but our children are here with us."

Bill and Heather put a lot of value on the family being together. Their lifestyle now makes it possible for them to enjoy their children more. In fact, the children can now come to work with them.

If you have children and are debating whether or not to make a move, some of the things to consider are:

1. How much quality time do you have as a family? Is your home like Grand Central Station or is it a nurturing environment?

2. Are you putting in so many hours at work that you aren't seeing your children grow up?

3. Are your family-oriented values being satisfied or are you just paying lip service to them?

4. Is it possible for you to make a lifestyle change without making a physical move?

Parenting is wrapped with a tight value system—one that can give parents guilt feelings. Numerous times, my mother has told me how bad she and Dad felt when they had to sell the dairy just at the point that I was moving toward taking it over. "I regretted for years that we had taken away your form of livelihood right when you were wanting to go to college and getting ready to start."

My feeling is, thank heavens they sold those cows! I hated getting up at 5:15 every morning to milk those cows, and then having to do it again at 5:15 in the evening—day after day, month after month. Even now, 30 years later, I still am so happy when 5:15 comes and I don't have to go milk.

The lifestyle you are considering may mean a fuller life for your children than the one they have now. You may have more quality time together. Take a serious look at all your priorities. Are any of them keeping you from experiencing a good family life? For example, putting a high priority on being the president of a company may not be compatible with spending quality hours with your children. If you are overly concerned about making sure the kids have everything they need, you may be working so hard to make money that you become a checkbook to your children, not a parent.

It is clear that some families are better off after making a lifestyle change that includes a move, while in other cases, the children find it difficult to adapt. "When making a move, it is important for the family to spend a lot more intentional time with each other," said minister Allen Nesbitt. "Sometimes when you move into a community, you get very busy doing things and the family takes a back seat.

"The children might be angry about having to leave their friends. The daughter might be thinking she can't be a cheerleader now and the son concerned about having to change football teams. When the kids are having a lot of difficulty, I recommend counseling to help them through the change. People are often surprised at how emotional the change can be. The counseling will help the kids work through any anger they may be holding inside."

As you plan your lifestyle change, make a list of the issues you are dealing with. Evaluate how these issues relate to your value system. Let your mind be open to options. You want to make a decision that improves your quality of life—not one that decreases it.

CHILDREN'S CONCERN FOR PARENTS

When making a lifestyle change, you may have your children to consider on one side and your parents to consider on the other. Having discussed how your lifestyle change might affect your children, how might it affect your parents?

Rolland and his wife, Sharon, in their mid-40s, contemplated making a move from San Francisco to a small town in Montana. Both sets of parents lived close by and were disturbed by the thought of them moving away. Sharon said, "My parents were very upset about our even thinking about moving. They hated to think of their three grandchildren being so far from them. Their feelings put a damper on our making a move."

When Karen and I left for Africa, it was difficult to think about not seeing our parents for three years. We couldn't afford to fly back and see them, and they couldn't afford to come and see us. What if they got sick? What would we do then? Fortunately that never happened. If they had made an issue about our leaving, which they didn't, it would have been tough to leave.

If you believe strongly in not disappointing your parents, and your parents don't want you to move, you will need to explore some creative options. Such was the case with Sandra Timpton, 28. "My mother is living by herself. When I told her I was going to quit my sales job and move, she immediately started crying. I felt terrible. I really wanted to get out of the rat race and had been thinking of making a change for some time, but had never discussed it with her. While I am very independent in one sense, I really care about my mother's feelings.

"I took her to the resort town where I wanted to live. That helped some. Then I bought her a plane ticket so that whenever she decided, she could come and see me. I also promised her that I would call her regularly.

"I try to write her every week, besides phoning. This has helped in my being away. We actually have shared more feelings now that I am away than when I lived closer. She also can see how much happier and more relaxed I am, and that makes her happy for me."

Going the extra mile to communicate with your parents left behind is one way to help soften the disappointment of your moving. Also set specific times you will come back to visit.

As you deal with this issue, you may have different value statements come to mind:

"My parents have taken care of me; now I need to take care of them. . . ."

"I am only being selfish if I move against my parents' wishes. . . ."

"I only have one life to live, live it now. . . ."

Clara, 48, and her husband would like to make a lifestyle change to get away from the pressures of their office jobs. They have the money to do it but Clara is an only child and is concerned about her 82-year-old mother who is living alone. "As bad as I would like to make a change and go live in the mountains and open up a little shop, I couldn't do that to my mother. I just figure it is not meant to be at this time. I would hate for my mother to know that I am staying here because of her. It probably would make her feel guilty."

There is no easy answer to this issue. If you want to make a change and don't because of your parent(s), you may develop some bitterness. If you do make the move, you may feel guilty. Some have found it helpful to talk to a counselor who helped them to sort through their feelings. A counselor may also bring up options that weren't thought about earlier.

SUMMARY: THOUGHTS ON FAMILY CONSIDERATIONS

Family considerations can create some of the biggest emotional struggles when making a lifestyle change. When family is involved, it can either be a very smooth transition or it can be tense and frustrating. For it to be smooth it takes an openness to others' feelings and priorities. It is not something that one day you walk in and announce you decided to make a lifestyle change.

For a smooth transition, keep your spouse informed of the thoughts going through your head and ask how he/she feels about what you are thinking. As you get feedback, your initial response might be to defend your thinking. Instead, carefully listen to what is being said. Ask questions to help clarify what you heard.

When you make a change which involves your family members, they may have the feeling that you are only thinking about yourself and really don't care how they feel. They may think, "If you really loved us, then you wouldn't challenge us with the desire to change."

What often happens is one person sees all the good and the other party sees all the bad and then both hang onto their points of view. By taking things slow, by not expecting everyone to immediately agree with your thinking, by being willing to give on your part, little by little, a win/win situation can be obtained.

Pacing and timing is critical. Allow the seed of an idea to be planted and then start focusing on the fruits of the idea. If all the attention is focused on what is going to be given up with change, and nothing on what will be gained, it's hard to get excited about making a change.

To open up communications, diagram your pushing and opposing forces of change. Have everyone else do the same. This breaks big issues down into smaller parts. As each person explains what they wrote, listen without trying to impose your reasoning on them. You'll have your turn.

Because of the complexity of change as it relates to others in the family, it is often helpful to visit with a counselor to work through roadblocks. A counselor is able to ask questions that help unravel why you or others feel a certain way. In the back of your mind, for example, you might be thinking, "If my spouse really loved me, he/she would understand how important a lifestyle change is for my sanity." Through a counselor you may discover that it's not a matter of loving you or not. Rather it is the fear your spouse has about leaving old friends and trying to make new ones. Without the help of a counselor, you could have spent weeks dwelling on whether your spouse really loved you—missing the real issue at hand.

When children are involved, the question is whether the change will mess up the rest of their lives or make their lives better. From interviews, I found that parents are divided about what might happen. Those that have changed have found there are good results for their children. They also tell of the special attention they gave the kids during that transition time.

A blanket statement about whether a lifestyle change is good or bad cannot be made. For some children the change opens them up, while for others, it leaves them feeling insecure. Children within the same family react to change differently. The real issue is what you as a parent do to be sensitive to their transition and to help them work through new feelings. You do have control over the end result.

While the emphasis has been on family, it can also relate to any primary relationship. Some of you may not have a spouse, or children, or living parents, but you do have primary relationships that your change will affect. Any change affects the fabric of a relationship—sometimes it becomes better, sometimes worse. The disasters arise when people charge forth without being sensitive to those around them.

QUESTIONS AND ACTIVITIES

1. What concerns do you have with regard to how family members will respond to a lifestyle change? Write down what you *think* family members feel and then talk with them about it.

2. What do you see as your weaknesses when it comes to handling differences of opinions? How has that affected your relationship with your family?

3. What do you do to help keep the channels of communications open? In what ways would you like to be better at communications? What are you doing to help become a better communicator?

4. On a separate piece of paper draw the pushing forces and the opposing forces of change for you. Ask your spouse to do the same.

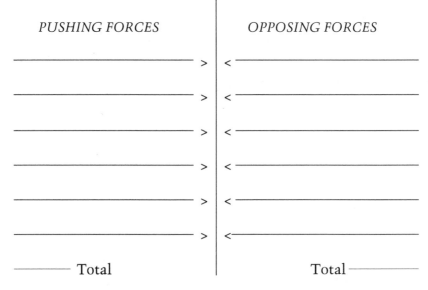

PUSHING FORCES   *OPPOSING FORCES*

——————————————— > < ———————————————

——————————————— > < ———————————————

——————————————— > < ———————————————

——————————————— > < ———————————————

——————————————— > < ———————————————

——————————————— > < ———————————————

———— Total   Total ————

After both of you have completed your lists, combine the two lists onto a common list. If you both have some of the same items, the item only has to be written down once. Make two copies of this last combined list.

Now, each of you take a copy of the combined list and give a value to each pushing and opposing force. Of all the forces listed, the most powerful one is given a value of ten and the least significant is given a value of zero. Since your spouse had some forces that may not affect you at all, you would give those a zero rating. There may be several forces with the same value ratings.

Add up the values for the pushing and pulling forces that you have just rated—spouse does the same on his/her sheet. Compare the ratings. Let this be a catalyst for discussing the differences of opinions and also the similarities.

5. Depending on the age of your children, it can be valuable to have the children participate in the above exercise, make their own lists and do some comparing.

OTHERS WHO MADE
LIFESTYLE CHANGES

Those who have already made lifestyle changes have insights that can make your change easier—that can help grease your slide for change. They can help you clear a mental path for pursuing your dreams. Their feelings of excitement, fear and adventure give new awareness and understanding to your feelings.

Although the following people have gone through different kinds of lifestyle changes, they shared a common inspiration of taking charge of their lives. As you read through their stories, ask yourself how would I have felt if that had been me? What would I have done differently? Even if you are not planning on making a major lifestyle change, you will gain insight on how to grease the slide for other types of change.

FROM PRESIDENT OF MAJOR COMPANY TO DEVELOPER OF MENTAL HEALTH AND DRUG ABUSE CENTERS

After Howard, 48, resigned as president of a major manufacturing company listed on the New York Stock Exchange, he had more time to look at his life values to discover what is truly important to him.

Since his resignation, he has taught some business college classes and is now actively involved in helping establish mental health and drug abuse centers. Notice how he looks at security, what values he considers to be important, what he has to say about change in his identity and how his family and friends reacted to his change.

"Resigning as president has given me a chance to look at what I want to do with the next chapter of my life— which I would say is 15 to 20 years long. My priorities have shifted in that I am more interested in doing something related to helping society in a more direct way, spending more time reading, being with the family, this type of thing—a lot different than during the hectic days of my presidential career. It has allowed me a new freedom to think and explore my values. We need to look at who we are and who we are serving and what we are here for.

"During the transition time there was a sense of relief that I was going to tackle this thing and head in another direction, but there was also a tremendous sense of fear and insecurity. There is a fear of losing your identity when you have patterned your life after certain things and measured your life progress in those terms, and likewise feel the people around you looked at you that way—including your family. Then what will I do with the rest of my life to give me the kind of identity that an individual needs? That whole process absorbed a lot of time and a lot of emotion and a lot of fear. It's important to keep in contact with your friends and others. The worst thing to do is to go into a shell, which is what most people do.

"What helped me move was my family. Once I started opening up to this whole thing and seeing the need to make a change and the circumstances driving me toward it, my family was ahead of me—that helped immensely.

"In working through the change, I sat down with a yellow pad and wrote down the pluses and minuses. In this kind of change, the minuses are: giving up some security of salary, giving up other kinds of security, the job, prestige, benefits and all these kinds of things. The positive things are that you relieve yourself of some of those tensions in terms of operating and running a business and thus open up your mind to other opportunities either in terms of running something else or in terms of contributing to society in a different way. Definitely the positive things of being able to do more reflection and spend more time thinking about some of the values of life and being able to spend more time with the family.

"Some people have treated me differently since the change and others haven't. I have been very pleasantly surprised that people have looked upon me as having talents in fields of expertise regardless of whether I was the president of a large company. In addition, I was able to sort out very quickly who were true friends from others that had been friends because of my title.

"A lot of people said they admired my courage to make a change. Some said they wished they had the financial security and all those things to make that kind of move. When you are almost 50 years old, you don't know how much financial security you have. That is a false kind of feeling. You can have a lot of dollars and lose them in a lot of different ways over a lifetime.

"Others would approach me and say, 'I wish I had the freedom to do what you did.' My answer to that is, 'Freedom is a relative thing.' Sure, if you have the resources it makes it easier than if you don't, but it's all relative and it's very illusionary."

When Howard was asked what advice he would give to others considering making a change, he said:

"Sit down and write out your goals and whether you are achieving them with what you are doing today or whether you need to make a lifestyle change in order to achieve them. Now if you are achieving most of the goals you are after, there wouldn't be a reason to change. You have to be very introspective with regard to goals, ambitions, where you want to head and how you want to do it. If you have your goals and objectives and priorities set right, over a period of time you will reach them by just persevering and not getting sidetracked. Select the career path that is in sync with your value system. Your whole belief system is your number-one priority and how consistent you are and how you practice it.

"Fear will keep people from making a change. Don't be afraid to change your career path if necessary. There was a time if you worked with one company for 30 years you might assume they were going to take care of you and everything would be fine. But with all the mergers and acquisitions and changes that are going on, that is not a very practical way to approach a working career anymore. I suggest you become adaptable to that and think creatively about that.

"Before the time of crisis, be sure you have thought through your value system because normally if you haven't, it's too late. If you haven't, your family may start fragmenting on you. You may go into some kind of withdrawal. You don't have time to think through your value system in times of crisis. Going to a professional counselor is very valuable in helping people sort out their thinking and clarifying their priorities and values.

"One final word—it is also important how you pick your friends and associates because they have a lot to do in steering you to a certain lifestyle and changes."

How are your friends and associates influencing your thinking about making a change?

Throughout his interview, Howard emphasized the importance of looking at your value system. For contentment in your life, it is important that your work is consistent with your value system. Do you feel your values and your life direction are currently in harmony with each other?

People are often reluctant to make a lifestyle change because they don't want to give up their security. Would you agree with Howard that security is relative? As you read his story, what insights did you get on your own situation?

Ph.D. MATH INSTRUCTOR BECOMES PAINTER

After eight years of teaching at the University of Montana, Mitch Billis, Ph.D., decided to pursue his love of painting. After making his transition, he said that if he had six months to live, he would be doing what he is doing right now. Can you say the same? Note his comments on materialism, jobs, free thinking and self-confidence. He continually stresses the importance of quality of life, not quantity.

Mitch's friends couldn't believe he was giving up lucrative job offers to go into painting full time. "I wouldn't trade my lifestyle for their ulcers," was Mitch's reaction.

"When my friends heard that I was going to leave my math career and go into painting, they thought I was crazy. They said, 'You could be doing anything, making a lot of money and you are giving all that up for painting.'

"I didn't think much about money when I got ready to change. I thought more about the quality of my life. Quality of life means to me the freedom to do what I want to do within the responsibilities that I have. I have always been aware of my mortality. If someone came up and said that I had six months to live and then asked if I would change my life, I would say 'No.' I would already be doing it. I don't want to have to change anything at the last minute. I am not sure where that came from, but it has always been the philosophy of my life.

"I had a friend that came out and visited me in Maine, and, after being there for three days, he could see why I gave up the high-paying opportunities to do what I am doing. I travel all over, including overseas. Even though I have to eat a lot of peanut butter sandwiches along the way, that is a small price to pay for the freedom I have.

"Beginning with sports in high school and college, I just feel that if I work hard enough I can accomplish anything I want to do. And that is one reason I probably don't spend a lot of time worrying about money. I know there is some way I can make it—I'll go pump gas if I need to.

"I see a lot of people caught in materialism, but that has never been my problem. I got over that real fast when I was younger. I don't know how I got over it, I guess I always appreciated freedom more than things. Maybe it was gearing my life toward accomplishing rather than collecting.

"I would like to ask people what is so important about a new car when you can have the freedom to live the way you want to live. The two things I have always wanted in my life were to do what I wanted to do and to have a sense of accomplishment. When people ask me what I want to do, I say, 'I want to love and I want to paint.' People are very important to me. I raised three of my four kids after getting a divorce.

"I don't understand why people don't look at their quality of life. I have a great friend who is a doctor. He is a great artist. He has got enough money to quit doctoring and paint, but he won't do it. Not doing it affects his life. It affects his relationship with his wife. It affects his relationship with his kids. It affects his relationship with himself, and yet, he just can't do it. It is almost like he is destroying his life because he won't change.

"Life is short. I am 49 now and I was 35 when I started painting. I want to live my life in a certain way. It is more of a process than a product. It's like Montaigne said, "It's the journey, not the arrival that matters." I am interested in the journey and not where I end up. I am not worried about whether or not I am going to end up with two cars.

"I want to be sorry for what I have done, not for what I haven't done. I feel it is better to take a wrong direction, than no direction at all. I would encourage people to take a step in any direction, just kind of think about what you might want to do and go in that direction. Take your life in your hands and go do it. By taking a wrong direction you will learn something. It may be that you don't want to do that particular thing, but along the way you may see something you will want to do. It will give you some ideas about what to do in your life."

If you had only six months to live, would you want to be doing what you are doing now? Are you like the doctor Mitch described who would be happier if he made a change, but wouldn't do it? Why are you afraid to make a change? Can you identify with Mitch's fear of remaining still? What a contrast with others who fear making changes. His life reflects the opportunity around us if we just walk through the door. As he says, even if you make a mistake, you will learn something. The important thing is to act. How are you going to feel if you go through life being a thinker rather than a doer? Will you be wondering how your life would have been different if you had?

THE MILLION-DOLLAR LIFESTYLE CHANGE

Would you be willing to give up a million dollars to have a higher quality of life? Yes? No? After getting a whack on the side of the head, Bob and Linda Heath answered yes to that question. During their interview, Bob spoke of the importance of Linda's support, how he felt about their spending habits, his strong involvement in the community and the importance of putting action behind words. Although Bob's life demonstrates the value of adaptive thinking, he knows how easy it is to put things off until that special day. His dad's life proved it.

"My dad was always telling me what he was going to do when he retired—but he died when he was 56 and never got to do any of those dreams. He was in the same business I had been in for the past 20 years. This made me decide to quit the company and change our lifestyle. It came as a big surprise to the company. They told me I would be giving up a profit-sharing plan that would be worth a million dollars in seven years.

"That got my attention. When I told Linda, she said, 'In seven years you might be dead, and what use is a million dollars if you can't spend it. Besides, I never planned on being a millionaire anyway.' We decided to slow our lives down—money, power, prestige wasn't everything. It wasn't worth it to give up for one's life.

"We wanted to travel; our house was as big as we ever dreamed of. We decided we would rather take what we have and move to some place where our quality of life would be less stressful.

"We made a long list of pluses and minuses. We asked what would be the worst thing that could happen. The worst thing that could happen would be to lose all our money. Another worst would be if the kids hated it. We decided that if for some reason it didn't work out, I could always start up another tire store.

"One of the big pluses was that Linda really felt I needed to slow down. A lot of women get into materialism and expect a high style of living. If the husband said, 'Why don't we go back to where we started, I think they would jump up and down and leave. If Linda hadn't been 120 percent behind me, I probably wouldn't have done it. I would have probably thought, okay, I should be a real husband and stay here and make the money that I know I can make.

"I am the kind of guy who was raised by a family that says you stay with one job and you don't make changes—you act responsibly. I had been ingrained that way. My dad worked for Western Electric for a number of years. It was almost like a death when he changed over from that job to the tire business because it was like he wasn't acting responsibly—you did a job and you stayed with a job and it didn't matter if you liked it. You needed to continue to show the manager you were responsible—get there early, leave late.

"When we got ready to move, I was flabbergasted that we owed over $43,000 beyond our house mortgage. I thought, Bob you are a fool. Finances definitely had gotten out of hand. We had gotten into the habit of spending the annual bonus before we got it. I remember in 1976 when we got a light bill for $500. That seemed like a terrible waste. We had a big house with a swimming pool and it took a lot of money to keep everything going—too much.

"I gave up over a million to make the lifestyle change. I can't say I never look back thinking about having all that money in my pocket. But the way we were spending, if I had waited to get that million, by then we would have probably owed another million so I wouldn't have gotten ahead.

"I was 40 at the time and some of the people sort of made fun of me saying that I was going through the 40-year-old syndrome. They thought I was crazy. They said we would be back in two years—but we weren't. Some of our close friends were upset with our leaving. Now most of them have also moved.

"We came to the mountains without jobs. Even though we did have some money from the business sale, it was a little scary. For two years we didn't do anything in particular except fix up an old house. After the first two years, I was really getting scared about my own intelligence. Linda kept saying, 'You can do anything,' but I was wondering if I could do anything but run a tire store."

Bob's confidence was reaffirmed when he took up real estate and became the top producer in the office.

"Our kids really enjoyed living up here. We had one son getting ready for college, a daughter who was eleven and another who was nine. I grew up in the same little house and had the same little circle of friends. Linda moved all over and felt the move would be good for the kids. It would help them learn what's on the other side— how to make adjustments.

"It's easy to talk about making a change, but something else when it comes to actually doing it. Some people settle into security. Some of our finest hours were when we didn't have a penny. We all run after security. That's dumb in my opinion. If you lose everything you've got, you can start over again. Look at the people who come over here from foreign countries with nothing—they make it.

"People need to put more fun in their lives. Don't do what all the other Americans think you should do. Have some fun—like kids. Kids go out and do those crazy things. Adults don't do things like that. Think what you would do if you were a kid again.

"If I died today and didn't get to the 65 retirement, I have already had more fun than most have had. If I die today, my family will have enough. I have given my kids a lot of confidence that they can do what they want to do.

"Americans are born with the gift of success—but they don't realize it. Lifestyle change may not be for everyone, but there are moves people can make that will give them twice the quality of life."

Linda's Comments

Linda now has her own jewelry store. While she recognizes the value of changing their lifestyle to get back to basics and to help Bob have a longer life, little by little she is beginning to see them falling back into some of the same lifestyle traps they were in nine years ago. The difference is that now they are aware of traps in the early stages.

"I really think we lengthened Bob's life by many years because he was living the very same lifestyle his dad was and his dad kicked over at 56. Strong man—never was sick—no one ever dreamed it could happen. I could have led the same lifestyle forever for all I had to do was to keep things going at home so Bob could do what he needed to do at the company. That was a full-time job for me.

"I remember when Bob got out of college and interviewed with this tire company. He said, 'I am going to work for them and I am going to stay with them for five years—even if it kills me.' And there were many times as a young man that he wanted to quit. However, his family background was such that you were thought to be a failure if you skipped from one job to the next.

"We lived in a big house. I loved my house. We had built it five years earlier and had done a lot of entertaining. But I was ready to move. Dump the big house and get a little house. We went from 3,850 square feet to 1,450 square feet. We got rid of a lot of furniture and things to move here.

"I don't have anything that I couldn't give up. You might be blessed more if you have that attitude.

"I think our kids thought we were rich. We had that big house with a big swimming pool. We were living higher and higher all the time—and we were spending it faster. I thought it would be better for the kids if we stepped back and became more basic.

"I was fortunate not having to work when raising the kids but you really don't get the chance to see your talents as a housewife. To be able to branch out really improves the quality of your life. It puts some fun into your life.

"We moved up here to slow down a little but sometimes I think we might need to move again. We have been here for nine years and we are really getting busy again. We have started to spend a little outside our means and I am determined to have all our bills caught up by the end of the year. Sometimes I feel it is all catching up with us again."

Bob and Linda felt their lives were out of control before their lifestyle change. Nine years later, it is beginning again. That is an important warning. If you are not careful, you will tend to bring some of your bad habits with you. What habits would you like to get rid of through your lifestyle change? Can you start getting rid of your undesirable habits before you start the change? How do you feel your life would be different if you got rid of them?

Some people accused Bob of going through a midlife crisis. I feel this is an unfortunate catchall label. Have you ever been given a label that you felt lumped you into a big category, overlooking your individualism? Labels can affect your thinking and decision making more than you realize. The more you understand your emotions and reasons for doing something, the less you will be threatened by off-the-cuff comments, such as "You are going through a midlife crisis," or "You are a job-hopper," or "You are a dreamer." You will have the assurance of knowing yourself regardless of what others say.

FROM PRESTIGE TO FULFILLMENT
FOR MOTHER AND SON

After her divorce, Susan Francis felt it important to get out of the city and rear her son, Jordan, in a small town of 1,200. "I feel that kids who grow up in rural communities grow up with more common sense," she said.

"People were surprised that I actually gave up my beautiful home, the live-in maid I had for six years, and moved. They called me a gutsy lady because of where I chose to reside. I just found a place I would like to live and raise my son and I don't call that gutsy—it's doing what I wanted to do.

"It was good for me to get away from my Dallas setting. I was spending too much on clothes, too many social events and stuff like that. As far as somebody wrapped in the social whirl, that got plastic to me. The things that were important to the ladies who I associated with in doing charity work were not into it for the charity, they were in it because they wanted their picture in the newspaper that next weekend. Not to say there weren't a lot of really neat ladies who were doing it, but that was just sort of my feeling on it.

"I wanted to get away from the social trappings and more into a community at the grass-roots level. The community work I am involved in now has meant a lot to me. It has been rewarding and fulfilling. I have met a lot of people really fast. I feel that by getting involved in community work, I am bettering the community for my child as well.

"Since making my lifestyle change, I have had a lot more time to think about what is really important in life and what is important to me. I am into self-improvement and education—learning and searching for a lot of answers such as, 'Why am I here in this universe?' I now have more time to search for answers.

"I don't know, but I guess when I was in Dallas I thought I was pretty hotsy-totsy. I am not sure I thought of anybody except me. I was impressed with where I was living and pretty impressed with getting myself there—but I didn't want to be there after I got there. It seemed plastic. The cocktail talk seemed plastic. I wasn't sure people really cared about me as much as they did about the family I had married into. I would go somewhere without my husband and they wouldn't recognize me. All of a sudden I would be a blank face after I socialized with people for five or six years.

"Back in Dallas I saw a lot of wealthy ladies who were frustrated and didn't know what to do with themselves. If they hadn't had money they would have been forced to do something with themselves, but like them, things were too easy for me. I wanted to challenge myself. I think a lot of boredom comes from not having to make yourself productive if you have the wherewithal.

"It is easy to get sedentary in your activities and in your way of thinking. It would be easy for me to be sitting in the house in Dallas right now and doing my silly little things. It's easy not to be motivated and it takes some effort to push yourself—and that can apply to dieting, exercising, just anything.

"I can't imagine a person really wanting to do something and not doing it, so I guess it would have to be the fear of change. I don't know what causes fear. I have never been afraid of anything, so it is hard for me to relate to fear.

"My range of friends is much broader here. I have friends who are carpenters and sewage workers who I think just as much of as others in more prestigious positions. They are just as smart as the bank presidents and the doctors. It wasn't that I was a snob about that sort of thing before, I just was never in a position to associate or pal around with laboring people. And now it doesn't matter. It is what is in their heart and their head that makes them special—not their title.

"Some people hate to give up things in order to make a change. If you don't have to give up anything, I think that is the best position to be in, but if you do have to give up something to make the change, then it is a time to test the importance of that change. If whether I made my lifestyle change depended on whether or not I kept my mink, I would have sold it. If you feel you have to stay, figure out how to make your life better where you are now.

"We make our own happiness. I don't think I am happier here than there, nor was I happier there than at college when I was growing up. If I reflect back on my life, I have smiled my whole way through. I don't like being unhappy.

"Everything that happens in your life has a lesson to be learned. A person might say, 'If this horrible incident hadn't happened then my life would be better.' You need to bless whoever did you dirty for being the instructor of that lesson. Everything happens for a reason. Maybe that happened to give you the guts to say, 'I am going to go someplace else.'"

Would you agree with Susan that everything that happens in your life has a lesson? If so, what are some of the lessons that you have learned from earlier events that are helping you now? When you have an attitude that everything has a lesson, it helps to take away some of the pain of the event. Your attention focuses on how this will make you a better person.

Not everyone has the financial resources that Susan enjoys. Yet she admits that she has to make sure she is productive to bring in the money she needs. Some find it hard to give up their nice home or prestigious address, even though it might mean greater fulfillment for them. Is that you?

SELF-CONFIDENCE REPLACES SECURITY TRAP

Wilting away in front of their TV set was not the way Bill and Myrna Ebert wanted to spend the rest of their lives. "People who do this have limited their horizons. They are living on this game board and never go past the edge. That is not the way we want to live our lives," was Myrna's explanation of why they made a lifestyle change four years ago when they both were in their mid-50s.

Before making the change, "We were looking for security and looking for someone else to make the decisions for us," Bill recalled. "That has all changed now."

This couple has more enthusiasm for living since taking charge of their lives. Building self-confidence enabled them to move ahead. Listen to them discuss their feelings about security, money, and what opened their eyes to new opportunities.

"Bill and I normally took a walk in the evening before going to bed. Ninety-seven percent of the houses we walked by, you could see people glued to their TVs. More and more of our friends were narrowing down their lives playing bridge. We wanted to continue to be active. The older you get, the harder you have to work at being active. We were 55 at the time and were in a frame of mind we weren't going to retire and be sedentary. If we were going to retire, we were going to retire into active life."

While Bill and Myrna were ready for a lifestyle change, the decision took some serious thinking. Bill had the security of 25 years of corporate life and Myrna had a very successful real estate business. They now have a retail clothing store which Myrna manages. Bill is kept very busy working with his son in the real estate appraisal business.

"I received a number of promotions, but the additional money never went as far as we expected it to," Bill said. "We kept saying, 'We ought to do something on our own. We ought to be in business for ourselves.'

"There were some things happening in my particular area of the corporation which made us a little apprehensive. We started doing some serious thinking. We went through a growing period in which we learned a lot about self-esteem, doing things for yourself, taking risks, stepping forward, going for it. This new knowledge was the impetus for our determining that we were going to do something. We didn't know what, and we didn't know where, but we were open to change.

"We had talked about selling everything in Wisconsin and moving to the mountains and doing our thing. But we realized that when you make a move you bring yourself with you. If you don't feel good about yourself before the move, you won't feel good after the move. You are going to lead the same lifestyle you left. It isn't going to change because you haven't changed. We see couples who are having marriage problems and they think making a move will help. It doesn't. You have got to change. The books, tapes, motivational speakers, all helped us do that."

"After you spend so many years with a major corporation, your thinking is capped. You are always waiting for someone else to make a decision—waiting for instructions to come down. You have to get away from it all and say, 'I can make decisions for myself.' I don't have to have the security of the corporation paying my insurance or my retirement plan. We've made more money here than I ever thought we would—and we are our own bosses and living where we want to live."

Myrna recalled how, "Before making our lifestyle turning point, we weren't that aware of how insecure we were. We were just going along with the things that presented themselves, doing what average Americans do. Then we started to dream about bigger things and dared to face some of our desires that we had always kept submerged. Before, they always seemed beyond our realm of reality. We started to open up our thinking—saying, 'Yeah, I really would like to take a trip to Europe.'

It was a kind of goal setting."

Bill had one regret. "I wish I had done something with my life at an earlier age so I would have been a better role model for my kids." Myrna added, "We get a lot of encouragement from our children. They are probably our biggest fans. They are so encouraging and supportive. All six are behind us 100 percent."

"A lot of people don't know they are stuck. Their lives have been so mediocre, they are just going to die mediocre and not realize there is a lot of color beyond their little cell. We have taken the lid off our future."

Do you ever feel that you are stuck in a prison cell? That you are not seeing all the color that exists? Do you feel that there's a lid on your future?

If you feel you can't follow your dreams, Bill and Myrna provide a testimony that it can be done. Their lives prove the importance of feeding your mind daily just as you feed your body. This book is food for the mind.

NEW LIFESTYLE, NEW INSIGHTS— SAME ADDRESS

Most of the people interviewed for this book made a geographic move when they made a lifestyle change. Leonard Burton did not. When Leonard, 40, sold his very successful Buick car dealership, most people were surprised. The dealership had grown to become the eleventh largest in the nation. From a pool of 4,000 Buick dealers, he was one of four asked to be on the General Motors President's Dealer Advisory Council in 1986. Despite this impressive track record, Leonard chose to switch to a lifestyle with less pressure. While Leonard stays very busy with his position on the city council, he no longer has a "regular" job. He and his wife, Boo, have discovered how much importance society puts on whether or not you have a job. "People look at you differently," he said. Although he is the same person, has the same friends and the same address, Leonard now has new insights.

Many people dream of the day they won't have to go to work anymore. Leonard, however, has found, "It's not as easy to relax as you think it's going to be, particularly after years of being programmed to get up and go to work. Things are different. You're the same person; you just don't have a job. You answer interesting questions when you go in to write a check and they ask for your business number and you don't have one. That's disquieting.

"Even though I am on the Irving [Texas] City Council, and even though I'm the same person, and I comb my hair the same way, and I wave at people the same way, and I wear the same clothes, I'm having trouble evaluating myself as a contributor. I think there is a little bit of stigma attached to Leonard Burton now—he's a goof-off, he's a playboy, the only thing he is doing right now is getting involved in civic activities. People always want the right kind of people involved in civic activities—those with jobs.

"When making a lifestyle change, be ready for numerous questions from people trying to figure out what it is you are now doing. With their curiosity, they are going to try to figure out if you can afford not to work—and for how long, or if you just can't find a job.

"The initial reaction is to flush a little bit when exposing to somebody you are unemployed. It leaves you standing real naked and vulnerable. After getting over the initial shock, something rushes through your mind—since you can afford it, tell them you are retired.

"Ultimately, I tell them I am in investments or I tell them I have my own company. I skirt the issue so I don't have to get into an in-depth discussion with every man on the street who wants to know whether I have any money in my checking account. All this starts working on you after about the 40th time you get asked what you are doing now."

While Leonard enjoys his freedom and being able to spend more time with his family, it is an adjustment not to be in the competitive business world. He is beginning to find his stomach churning the same way it did when he still owned his business. "The discomfort is starting to come back. The best I can figure out, there must be some kind of window of time that's all right to be between jobs. If there is a 10-point scale of time that it's socially acceptable to be without a job, I've passed five and am heading for 10. There is a pressure to do something or at least know what I am going to be doing. Until I know the answers for that, the knots get bigger and bigger in my stomach."

Leonard's lifestyle change has moved him out of the high-pressure situation he was in. Now he's looking for a business with challenges but less pressure.

His wife, Boo, had this to say about their lifestyle change:

"It is just one of the very best things that's ever happened to us. I almost feel guilty sometimes that we are in such a nice position in that we don't have pressure to go back and seek daily employment. I feel a whole lot better that he responded so well physically since his stress is gone.

"As far as having him around home, it has been wonderful! Up until the time we sold the business, we didn't have the time we wanted to devote to the family. This has been the perfect time for this to happen with our boys who are 12 and 14.

"I just don't want to be 60 to 70 years old, and look back at my life and say, 'Gee, I wish we'd have tried that.' I think there is nothing sadder than a person or a family that somehow cheats themselves out of something. I think life was meant to be lived and enjoyed. I think if you spend a lot of time determining the reasons you want to do something, and if the reasons seem valid, then go for it. I feel this whole experience has made me a little bit more broad-minded as to what other people are doing with their lives."

Selling the car dealership marked a major lifestyle change in Leonard and Boo's lives. Since they didn't move, they were surrounded by friends whose lifestyles had not changed. These friends raised a number of questions. How would you respond if everyone kept questioning you about what you were doing? Eventually someone would give you the impression that they felt you had lost your mind to have made such a change. How would you respond to that accusation? If you scale your life down by stepping out of a high-pressure position or selling your business, be ready for those on the sidelines to play Monday-morning quarterback.

The stronger your confidence and the better you understand and abide by your value system, the less you will be bothered by remarks from the sidelines. You will be living your life, not someone else's.

BREAK OUT OF THE COCOON

Making a lifestyle change is more than an event—it's an approach to life. Dick Hauserman made his change in 1961—back before lifestyle changes were as prevalent as they are in the 1980s. Dick, now 70, reflected on the change he made when he was 45. "I wouldn't change it for the world. I have had wonderful, thrilling experiences and they are still going on today."

The past 25 years have given Dick new insights on success, failure and what it takes to break out of a cocoon. While he is glad he made his change, he can see why people stay stuck in their cocoons.

"When I was in my 20s, I spoke of changing my occupation when I became 45. By coincidence, at 45 I got a call from Vail, Colorado, to help develop a resort there. At the time of the call, I was in charge of marketing for the Hauserman Company. The job was a rat race—traveling 175,000 miles a year, visiting a different branch nearly every week of the year.

"My father died of a heart attack at the age of 58, and I had a tendency toward high cholesterol. The doctor said, 'If you keep this up, sooner or later you will have serious deterioration in your health.' When the opportunity came to get out of the rat race and take part in developing a resort ski city, it was an easy answer. I was on the first board of directors of Vail and was also the chairman of the executive committee. It was terribly exciting.

"When I resigned from Hauserman Company in Cleveland I think everyone was surprised that, at that stage of life in a very good job with infinite potential, I would take a gamble on something that didn't even exist.

My brothers lived in Cleveland, belonging to the same social set, spending time with the same people year after year. My leaving all of that was difficult for them to understand.

"Some people don't need to change. They are very happy where they are. They are intelligent, hard-working people. They travel, they have close friends, and within their little cocoon they have lots of activities. I wouldn't swap my life for theirs.

"I clearly remember my feelings when my wife and I left our home in Cleveland and headed for our new life in Vail. It was a four-day drive and I kept thinking, we have cast off and we are afloat. I was confident, however, that Vail would be a success even though lots of people thought I was crazy.

"All my life I have felt somewhat insecure as far as competing with others. I always dreaded taking an exam because I thought I might fail. I never did, but I was afraid I would. I have always been a little bashful in certain respects—until I became familiar with whatever it was. Then I wasn't."

Although Dick sees himself as bashful, he is on a first-name basis with a number of national celebrities. It's hard to believe he has a bashful bone in his body. Have you ever met someone who sees himself as shy, yet plows right ahead without fear?

"When I played football in college," Dick recalled, "my coach said, 'The team that makes the breaks, gets the breaks.' When things happen, you take advantage of them and go ahead. You take a little chance. You don't sit back and do nothing.

"I have gotten involved in projects and lost money. While it may feel like the end of the world, it isn't. You have to say to yourself, capitalize on your disaster. Usually you will find a way. It may be a very depressing time, but remind yourself that if you have faith and your health, you can do anything.

"I have been very fortunate in my life to have some very close friends who have been very inspirational to me.

Lowell Thomas was one. Another is Phillip Johnson, who is one of the most famous architects alive today. He was saying that his decade of the 70s—he was 79 at the time—was one of the greatest times in his life. I needed to hear that, for when I turned 70, it was very depressing for me."

Do you remember some of those feelings when you hit certain birthdays and you got the feeling you were old? How did you handle it?

Dick was driving back from Los Angeles and saying to himself, "I'm 70. I'm old. I'm a senior citizen. I didn't know how I was going to handle it. Then I decided I wasn't going to let it bother me. Why be 70 if you don't feel 70? Who was I kidding? I wasn't kidding anyone, but, nevertheless, again it goes back to health. If you feel good and you have the energy, why not use it?"

Throughout the interview, Dick brought up the importance of health. Unfortunately, many people have a lifestyle that is hurting their health. Health is one of those things we often don't appreciate until it is too late. Dick believes that if you have your health, it will help you do anything you want. To keep your health you need to pace yourself.

"A message I would pass on to others is to slow down. A lot of things that keep us so occupied aren't really that important. You can live a lot longer if you don't beat yourself into the ground. Pace yourself.

"Men get so tied up with their businesses, they don't take time for their wives, their families. This is unfortunate because I feel women deserve a lot more attention and credit than they get. Men need to pace their lives so they have more time for their families."

Dick's major lifestyle change started 25 years ago. It has opened the door to new experiences and adventures. His life has touched people from all walks of life. His advice is sought and respected by his friends—such as his good friend, former astronaut Scott Carpenter, who asked Dick what he should do with the rest of his life. Dick's advice—"Make use of your speaking ability and take time to ski"—was accepted.

Do you feel as if your life is in a cocoon? Why? Are you pacing yourself? Are you taking time for your family and friends? What are you planning to do to make more time for them? Health is terrifically important for quality living. Do your diet, exercise plan and other habits reflect your sincere interest in living a fuller life? Or are your health habits on hold? Your life and your energy level are in your hands—regardless of your age.

IT'S UP TO YOU

This book has introduced you to people and ideas directed at helping you take your life off hold. You now have the tools to implement a lifestyle change. Tools that will put new vigor in your life. Ideals and thoughts that become the seeds of a new life of greater fulfillment. A life open to change.

Like some of your parents, perhaps, my dad has always enjoyed gardening. At 74, he still has the biggest garden in the neighborhood—and he gives everything away. I got my first lesson in gardening when I was three. Like any young boy, I wanted to be like Dad.

Very methodically, Dad showed me the colorful little packages of seeds with pictures of peas, carrots and lettuce on them. Patiently he explained how to prepare a nice soft bed for the seeds to sleep in. He marked out a patch that I could call my garden. Taking a hoe, which looked huge back then, I carefully prepared the seedbed. After I decided what I wanted to grow, Dad showed me how to plant the seeds.

Each morning I sprinkled the ground with water, hoping that something would hurry up and start growing. Finally, a little carrot sprig was seen. Then there were more and more. Along with the carrots came the weeds. I took the big hoe and chopped away at the weeds. It was hard to control the big hoe. Eventually, half of the spindly carrot tops got chopped off. After a while, I learned that it was better to pull the weeds out by hand or dig them up with a kitchen spoon.

Today that whole experience reminds me of life. We have a mental seedbed. Whatever we plant will come up—providing the seeds are fed. We have tools to help get rid of the weeds around our delicate seedlings, but if we are not careful we can chop off the seedlings as we get rid of the weeds. This is just the beginning of the analogy—you can expand it to describe your own life.

Ninety-two-year-old Bernice Anderson has a recipe for building a good attitude. "There's no denying that we oldsters have our low moments. We can either succumb to all this devastation or decide to accept it with as good grace as we can muster, while reminding ourselves that *inside* we're still the selves we've always been. We can keep our interest in other people and do as much as we possibly can for any who need cheering. We can keep up our interest in worthwhile projects. We can always simply refuse to allow any negative thought to take possession of our minds or to get the better of us."

GETTING PAST "YES BUT"

You have read how others have taken charge of their lives. Does that give you faith that you too can do it? If it has been done once, it can be done again—and you can do it!

The very fact you have read this far suggests that you are serious about finding a new path for your life—one that has quality and sparkle to it. Are you having trouble taking that first step? Why? What could be said or done that would help you?

Are you like Sharon Muse, who, after reading some of the pages for this book, said "I can see how those people made a change, but their situation is different." This is a case of "YES BUT." During the discussion that followed, Sharon admitted that she lacked faith in herself. She compared her feelings to wanting to get to the other side of a river, jumping in, struggling and having to turn back.

After evaluating the forces pushing her toward change and those holding her back, she recognized she really didn't know what she wanted to do. While she wanted to make a change, changing for the sake of change is risky. It is important to have a goal and then systematically plan the steps needed to reach it. Do you have a goal you are truly excited about? Or is your goal to just get out of where you are right now?

After Jim Frye read this book he said, "You make it sound as if making a lifestyle change turns everything into a bed of roses. I think life has a lot of disappointments and you should put more of that in your book. All this stuff about having a positive attitude and having confidence is good, but it's not that easy." Another "YES BUT."

People tend to have a filter system that blocks out what their belief system is not prepared to accept. A negative person only hears the negative. Every negative thing that happens, every failure, every disappointment, reinforces their view of life. In turn, that reinforcement gives them a feeling of being right. It gives them a way to explain why things have gone badly in their own lives. They would rather be right than happy.

A negative person is very suspicious of positive people. Positive people are seen as having their heads in the clouds, hiding their true pain, not in touch with reality. Positive suggestions given to negative people are usually answered by "YES BUT."

Would you describe yourself as a positive person? How many times did you say "YES BUT" as you read this book? If you are stuck, that may be the reason. There is nothing wrong with stopping to evaluate how new information applies to your life, but that's different than discrediting a statement with "YES BUT."

IT'S IN YOUR HANDS

You have the tools. It's up to you to use them. Some people will tell about a book they've read or a speaker they've heard, but when asked how it affected their life, they will admit they haven't changed. It is too easy to just remain the same.

When I was a kid I joined the 4-H softball team. I didn't really enjoy it, but it was the macho thing for a 10-year-old to do. Based on my athletic ability, it could have been questioned if I was more help to my team or the other team—my athletic talents remained hidden.

In one of the big games we were behind in the last inning with runners on first and second. Coach Molzen looked down the bench and, with a shocked look on his face, realized I hadn't played yet. In the 4-H league, every player had to play at least once during the game. He called me over and told me to bat after the next batter. I was nervous and excited. I took a handful of bats and beat them on the ground like the pros. I picked out a shiny black one, walked over to Coach Molzen and asked, "Do you think I can make a home run with this bat?" With a hopeful look in his piercing German eyes he said, "It's in your hands."

What you do with the rest of your life is in your hands. Therefore you have to be accountable. That's good and bad news. The bad news is that when things go wrong, you have to ask yourself what you did to cause that. You can't blame your boss, spouse or kids. The good news is that you are in the driver's seat. You are not a passenger going along for the ride, being taken wherever the driver decides to go.

Hopefully you don't feel like the people who described their lives as like:

" . . . a bumper car at an amusement park, getting pushed around from all directions."

" . . . a ball in a pinball machine running into one obstacle, then another, then getting slapped by the flippers on the side."

" . . . a leaf floating on a lake getting blown from side, to side, to side."

These are hopeless feelings that keep people stuck. The more you are convinced that you are in control and that your life is in your hands, the more excitement you will have about living. If you aren't in control, who is? How can you change that?

In my management consulting, I find employees who spend far too much time pointing their fingers at someone else. Have you ever noticed that when you point your finger at someone, there are three fingers pointing back at you? When a glitch arises, ask yourself, "What did I do to cause that to happen and what can I do to prevent it from happening again?" That is being accountable. Even though you may feel no responsibility for what happened, keep looking in the mirror.

A lot of us tend to want to blame others, nature or the economy for our plight. Then there are people like my nephew

Brian Wiens who, after losing a leg in a tragic motorcycle accident, spent months in physical therapy so he could play football again. Perhaps you saw the October 1981 United Press International article about the one-legged football player from Kansas. He chose not to be stopped by tragedy.

While events do happen in our lives that we feel are out of our hands, how we react to those events *is* in our hands. Maybe the company you worked for has shut down after 25 years and you now are looking for another job. You can get mad, you can cuss at your boss, you can blame the economy, or you can look at this as a new beginning for something even better. For every minute you waste blaming someone else, you are one minute further behind in taking charge of your life.

Whenever I feel depressed or stuck, I take long walks or go swimming. The physical activity helps me over the hump. After I was fired there were a number of nights I took some very long walks until finally I walked through that painful door of my life and started getting excited about an even brighter future. I kept telling myself, it's in my hands. Whenever I wanted to sit in the corner and pout I knew it was time to take another walk.

Tough experiences can be the reset buttons for our lives or they can blow the fuse. It's not what happens to you, it's what you do that sets the stage for the next chapter of your life.

DO IT NOW

Why wait another day to take your life off hold? I hope that by now, the juices are flowing to help you take charge of your life. To help get started, begin by doing the one thing you dread the most. Break the ice. Be driven by challenges, not stopped by fears. Start planning now. Start asking questions now. Start exploring options now. What do you think you will gain by waiting?

You have only one life to live. The rest of your life begins right now. I wish you much success in your lifestyle change.

WHAT I LEARNED FROM WRITING THIS BOOK

I learned that materialism is a much bigger trap than I first suspected.

I learned that the average person has a lot more insight into life than some experts give him or her credit for.

I learned that the voice of experience is more valuable than the voice of intellectualism.

I learned that people spend a substantial amount of time justifying why they are stuck where they are right now.

I learned that people pay lip service to a better quality of life, then sacrifice their health and families to have another Mercedes.

I learned that savvy is a function of experience and not age. Some young people have a lot to teach the gray-haired, if they would just listen.

I learned that people who have taken charge of their lives use a different vocabulary to describe their lives than those who are wilting with age and sameness.

I learned that, regardless of what you say, if another person isn't willing to change, you are wasting your breath.

I learned that one of life's main motivators is having a sense of purpose and meaningful direction. Without that, life can be boring and depressing.

I learned that some people would rather be unhappy where they are than risk change.

I learned that more and more people are starting to focus on the quality of life, not just the quantity.

I learned that some people make a lifestyle change because of their children and others don't make a change because of their children.

I learned that some of my values are based more on social pressure than on my core beliefs.

I learned that when you get past the facades that make us socially acceptable, we all have a lot in common.

SUGGESTED READING

Addington, Jack Ensign. *All About Goals and How to Achieve Them*. Marina del Rey: De Vorss & Company, 1977.

Bach, Richard. *Illusions: The Adventures of a Reluctant Messiah*. New York: Dell Publishing, 1977.

———. *Jonathan Livingston Seagull*. New York: Avon, 1970.

Bolles, R.N. *What Color Is Your Parachute?* Berkeley: Ten Speed Press, 1983.

Bolles, R.N., and John C. Crystal. *Where Do I Go from Here with My Life?* Berkeley: Ten Speed Press, 1980.

Bridges, William. *Transitions: Making Sense of Life's Changes*. Reading: Addison-Wesley Publishing, 1980.

Bry, Adelaide, and Marjorie Bair. *Visualization: Directing the Movies of Your Mind*. New York: Barnes & Noble Books, 1978.

Coleman, Carol, and Michael A. Perelman. *Late Bloomers: How to Achieve Your Potential at Any Age*. New York: Ballantine Books, 1987.

Frankl, Viktor, E. *Man's Search For Meaning*. New York: Pocket Books, 1939.

———. *The Unheard Cry for Meaning*. New York: Touchstone, 1978.

Gawain, Shakti. *Creative Visualization*. New York: Bantam Books, 1978.

Gore, Irene. *Add Years to Your Life and Life to Your Years*. New York: Stein & Day, 1973.

Hill, Napoleon. *Think and Grow Rich*. New York: Fawcett Crest, 1969.

Kushner, Harold S. *When All You've Ever Wanted Isn't Enough*. New York: Summit Books, 1986.

Lefkowitz, Bernard. *Breaktime: Living Without Work in a Nine to Five World*. New York: Hawthorn Books, Inc., 1979.

Maltz, Maxwell. *Psycho-Cybernetics*. New York: Prentice-Hall, 1960.

Mandino, Og. *The Greatest Salesman in the World*. New York: Bantam Books, 1968.

———. *The Greatest Miracle in the World*. New York: Bantam Books, 1975.

Maslow, A.H. *Motivation and Personality*. New York: Harper, 1954.

Neesenberg, Gerard. *The Art of Creative Thinking*. New York: Simon & Schuster, 1982.

Peale, Norman Vincent. *Enthusiasm Makes the Difference*. New York: Fawcett Crest, 1967.

———. *The Power of Positive Thinking*. New York: Prentice-Hall, 1954.

Peck, M. Scott. *The Road Less Traveled*. New York: Simon & Schuster, 1978.

Percy, Charles. *Growing Old in the Country of the Young*. New York: McGraw Hill, 1974.

Powell, John S.J. *Fully Human Fully Alive*. Allen, Tex.: Argus, 1976.

Rubin, Lillian B. *Women of a Certain Age: The Midlife Search for Self*. New York: Harper & Row, 1979.

Schenkel, Susan. *Giving Away Success*. New York: McGraw-Hill, 1984.

Schuller, Robert H. *Tough Times Never Last, But Tough People Do!* New York: Bantam Books, 1983.

Sheehy, Gail. *Passages*. New York: E.P. Dutton, 1976.

———. *Pathfinders*. New York: William Morrow, 1981.

Wonder, Jacquelyn, and Priscilla Donovan. *Whole Brain Thinking: Working from Both Sides of the Brain to Achieve Peak Job Performance*. New York: William Morrow, 1984.

Yankelovich, Daniel. *New Rules: Searching for Self-Fulfillment in a World Turned Upside Down.* New York: Random House, 1981.

Ziglar, Zig. *See You At the Top.* New York: Pelican, 1984.